SCOUNDRELS
═══ *of the* ═══
SALISH SEA

SCOUNDRELS
of the
SALISH SEA

TALES OF CRIME AND PUNISHMENT
IN WASHINGTON STATE'S HISTORY

CAROL TURNER

AMERICA
THROUGH TIME®
ADDING COLOR TO AMERICAN HISTORY

Cover photo by Roger Mosley.

America Through Time is an imprint of Fonthill Media LLC
www.through-time.com
office@through-time.com

Published by Arcadia Publishing by arrangement with Fonthill Media LLC
For all general information, please contact Arcadia Publishing:
Telephone: 843-853-2070
Fax: 843-853-0044
E-mail: sales@arcadiapublishing.com
For customer service and orders:
Toll-Free 1-888-313-2665

www.arcadiapublishing.com

First published 2020

Copyright © Carol Turner 2020

ISBN 978-1-63499-223-7

Typeset in 10.5pt on 13pt Sabon
Printed and bound in England

Acknowledgments

I owe an enormous debt to the noble folks who put historical newspapers online. I also owe thanks to Rodney Pedersen, City of Anadarko; Roger Mosley; Sabra Fawcett; Gregory Manning Fawcett; Laurie Ambrose; Mary Hammer, Washington State Archives; Julie Lundquist, Lake View Cemetery; Kris Kinsey, University of Washington Libraries; Oregon State Archives; Jewell Lorenz Dunn, Washington State Archives Southwest Regional Branch; Yasmin Ramada, Beinecke Rare Book and Manuscript Library, Yale University; Andy Erickson, CriticalPast Archival Footage; Stefan Freelan, The Spatial Institute, Huxley College of the Environment, WWU; Chas Turner; Jocelyn Turner; Richard Turner; Kena Longabaugh and Jamie Hardwick, Fonthill Media; and Alison Costanza, Washington State Archives Northwest Regional Branch.

Contents

I

Leschi and Quiemuth: War is Murder (1856)

Before the Treaty of Medicine Creek, Chief Leschi of the Nisqually traded regularly with white homesteaders and agents from the Hudson Bay company, communicating via Chinook jargon, the regional trade language. One white rancher owed Leschi his life, after the rancher and his cattle were washed downstream when trying to cross the Puyallup River. During the rancher's battle against the heavy current, Leschi appeared and got them safely across.

Leschi's older half-brother, Chief Quiemuth, also lived peacefully with their new white neighbors. The trouble began with the Treaty of Medicine Creek, negotiated in December 1854 by Territorial Governor Isaac Stevens. Stevens was also superintendent of Indian affairs of the territory, and his mandate as such was to procure as much prime farmland for white settlers as he could get his hands on.

The Medicine Creek treaty covered multiple tribes, including the Nisqually, Puyallup, Steilacoom, Squawskin, S'Homamish, Stehchass, T'Peeksin, Squi-aitl, and Sa-heh-wamish. The treaty was named after the creek where it was negotiated, which is now called McAllister Creek, apparently after one of the white men who featured prominently in the story of the Puget Sound War.

Both Quiemuth and Leschi signed the treaty with an "X," but some historians insist that at least Leschi's mark was forged. Either way, Leschi and many others were deeply disturbed by the terms of the treaty, once they understood what was in it. Traditional Nisqually lands lay along the Nisqually River and included prime farmlands where the tribe grew potatoes and other vegetables. Access to the river was vital since their staple diet consisted largely of salmon.

The treaty called for the Nisqually to leave their Nisqually River farmlands and relocate to a piece of land on a bluff that was not good for farming. They retained their fishing rights but their access to the river itself was blocked.

Leschi vowed to fight this treaty and traveled to Olympia to protest, but Stevens considered it settled. Under Leschi's leadership, the Nisqually refused to leave their farms. The refusal escalated into what became known as the Puget Sound War between the whites and the Nisqually, Muckleshoot, Puyallup, and Klickitat tribes. Leschi was the leader of this coalition.

Hostilities increased in the fall of 1855, and the war kicked into high gear in October of that year when nine white settlers, including a baby, were massacred at White River. The whites blamed Leschi for this attack, but he denied involvement and said it was the work of "*cultus*," Chinook jargon for "worthless fellows."

Also during October, a group of white volunteers called Eaton's Rangers was patrolling the same area. During two separate skirmishes where bands of Indians attacked the Rangers, four of the volunteers and an unknown number of Indians were killed. Again, the Rangers blamed Leschi and Quiemuth but it's not clear if they were present. Either way, both Leschi and Quiemuth became wanted men for the deaths of the four Eaton's Rangers.

In March 1856, on the Maschel Prairie (in today's Pierce County), white volunteer patrols killed a number of Indian non-combatants—primarily women, children, and the elderly. Historians disagree on the number killed—by some accounts between eight and thirty.

During this period, Governor Stevens forcibly removed a large number of Native Americans to Fox Island. As with many details surrounding the Puget Sound War, estimates on the number of those exiled to Fox Island vary wildly, from 500 to 4,000. Many of these people died of starvation or exposure. In January 1856, Leschi rowed to the island and met with James Swan, who was in charge of the internment camp there. Leschi was tired and wanted to end the war. He told Swan that he had been driven into the war but that his "heart was sick now" and would make peace. He said all he wanted was enough land to raise a few potatoes.

Word got out that Leschi was on the island and a steamship soon arrived carrying soldiers who wanted to "rescue" Swan and arrest Leschi. Swan prevailed on them to not escalate the situation. The steamship left but returned later with a howitzer, planning to take Leschi by force. However, Leschi had already gone.

A couple months later, the final battle took place. Referred to as the Battle of Connell's Prairie, about 150 Nisqually, Klickitat, and Yakama warriors engaged about 110 whites in a battle that went badly for the Native Americans. After this, they withdrew east over the Cascades, abandoning their old territory.

Life was extremely difficult in the eastern plains for the exiles. Game was hard to find and there were no salmon or potato crops to sustain them. In destitute condition, Leschi approached a white friend of his, Dr. William F.

Tolmie, an agent for the Hudson Bay Company, asking for ammunition. He said he needed it to hunt for food, not to wage war. He said he and his people were nearly starved.

A month later, in November 1856, Quiemuth appeared at the farmhouse of some friendly white settlers that he had known in the past. Quiemuth said that he wanted to surrender and face trial for the Eaton's Rangers deaths. He asked them to escort him to Olympia and protect him from vigilantes.

His friends agreed and the group set out that same night, reaching Governor Stevens's office in Olympia at 2:30 a.m. They awoke Stevens, who immediately arranged for an escort to take Quiemuth to Fort Steilacoom. Stevens then went back to bed.

At around 5 a.m., as the group was preparing to leave, a group of men burst into the governor's office. One of the men leveled a pistol at Quiemuth and fired. The men in the office fought back, and during the melee, Quiemuth was stabbed. As Quiemuth fell dead, the attackers escaped into the night.

Governor Stevens crawled out of bed again, demanding an explanation. The escort could not say who shot Quiemuth, who stabbed him, or how the vigilantes learned he was there. They did, however, identify one vigilante as Joseph Bunting, a son-in-law of Lt. James McAllister, one of the Eaton's Rangers who had been killed. The next morning, a coroner's jury declared that Quiemuth had been killed by "some person unknown to the jury."

Meanwhile, Leschi was camped with several followers in a secluded area in the upper Nisqually River. Two Indian bounty hunters approached his camp in a friendly manner, then took him captive and carried him on a horse to Fort Steilacoom. Officers escorted him to Olympia to face charges for killing one of the Eaton's Rangers, Abram Benton Moses.

During Leschi's trial, he insisted he was not in the area at the time of the attack. The testimony of a white volunteer, Antonio B. Rabbeson, formed the basis of the prosecution's case. He said that his group encountered a party of Indians, including Leschi and Quiemuth, and engaged in a long conversation with them. During this exchange, the Rangers asked the Indians if they knew anything about the burning of a house owned by a man named Connell, for whom Connell's Prairie was named. Rabbeson said Leschi suggested that the house had burned by accident. The Rangers then left and as they were crossing a swamp, the Indians attacked. Rabbeson said that he had been acquainted with Leschi for ten years and that he "believed" Leschi was the one who fired at Moses.

Another witness who was present at the battle testified for the defense. Andrew J. Bradley stated that he knew Leschi well. He described the encounter differently. He said that when the Rangers first spotted them, the Indians headed into the woods to avoid them. They called out to them, whereupon three of the Indians reappeared and they talked. Bradley said that one of his own party, a Dr. Burns, started a fight by grabbing a gun from one of the Indians.

He agreed that his group then left and headed into the swamp, and that they were attacked there. However, he said it was impossible to see who attacked them because of the gun smoke. He said he did not see Leschi at all during any part of the encounter.

Another defense witness, A. J. Simmons, testified that, before the trial, Rabbeson had told him he did not know who had attacked them in the swamp. Furthermore, Rabbeson had never mentioned knowing Leschi in the past. In short, Simmons said that Rabbeson was lying.

Dr. William F. Tolmie also testified for Leschi and described his friendliness and good relationship with the Bostons, as the Indians referred to white settlers, until Leschi felt his people had been cheated by the treaty.

When the trial went to the jury, they were unable to arrive at a verdict. In March 1857, they put him on trial again. Much of the testimony was the same at the second trial. This time, Leschi was found guilty of murder and sentenced to hang.

Leschi's supporters made numerous attempts to get him a new trial. His supporters and enemies circulated petitions for and against him. The defense appealed the case to the Supreme Court of Washington Territory, which upheld the guilty verdict. Meanwhile, his execution was scheduled for June 10, 1857.

After several delays, the day of Leschi's hanging arrived on February 19, 1858. A newspaper reporter wrote that Leschi looked very ill and weak as he arrived at the place of execution about a mile from Fort Steilacoom. He said Leschi ascended the scaffold with a "firm step, as if he desired to show the white man how fearlessly an Indian can meet death."[1]

Leschi made a statement, in Chinook jargon, that he would "soon meet his maker—that he had made his peace with God, and desired to live no longer—that he bore malice to none, save one man, and upon him he invoked the vengeance of heaven." They did not say who that man was.[2] Leschi's hanging was the first recorded case of capital punishment in Washington Territory.

Soldiers buried Leschi near the execution site, at the mouth of Muck Creek.

After the two-year Puget Sound War ended, the Nisqually won a better reservation, back on their farmlands along the Nisqually River, much of which remains intact today. On July 4, 1895, nearly thirty years later, members of the Nisqually reburied both Chief Leschi and Chief Quiemuth on the Nisqually Reservation.

Some 146 years after the hanging of Chief Leschi, on December 10, 2004, the "Historical Court of Inquiry and Justice," led by Chief Justice Gerry Alexander of the State of Washington, exonerated Chief Leschi of the crime of murder.

2

Attack at Ebey's Landing (1857)

Before the Salish Sea region was heavily settled by white homesteaders, fierce tribes from the north routinely paddled down south in search of plunder and slaves. Sometimes dubbed the Vikings of the Pacific Northwest, the warrior Tlingit and Haida people, who still live in today's southern Alaska and British Columbia, were referred to collectively by people around Puget Sound as the "Northern Indians."

In the year 1856, a large group of Northern Indians arrived in the Puget Sound area. They had travelled over 1,000 miles in gigantic canoes that could hold up to 100 warriors each. Area residents, both white and Salish, went on high alert due to the Northern Indians' fearsome reputation, penchant for taking heads as trophies, and kidnapping slaves.

This was the period of the Puget Sound War, and a U.S. Navy gunboat—the USS *Massachusetts*—had already sailed up from San Francisco to help "convince" dissenting Salish peoples to comply with treaties they did not agree with. Soon, the Navy would be called upon to fight the Northern Indians, who were considered an invading force from another country.

In April, a group of sixty or so Northern Indians landed at Port Townsend, but American sailors from the USS *John Hancock* quickly chased them off. The Northern Indians left but issued threats as they did so. Anxiety among locals increased drastically. In October, a party of Northern Indians attacked a schooner near Seattle, killing one. Other reports spread about attacks and robberies on the part of the Northern Indians. No one was sure where they were, but they were obviously still in the region.

In November, a large group of Northern Indians appeared at the settlement of Steilacoom. Terrified residents sent word to the U.S. Army at Fort Steilacoom, who contacted the USS *Massachusetts*. The *Massachusetts* hurried in that direction, but by the time they arrived, the Northern Indians had gone.

After getting word that the group had been seen heading north, the *Massachusetts* followed. The ship anchored that night at Apple Tree Cove at today's Kingston, then learned the Northern Indians were at Port Gamble.

Port Gamble was a logging community with a sawmill. A number of white settlers and S'Klallam, a Salish tribe, lived there and worked at the sawmill. When the Northern Indians arrived, the superintendent of the sawmill sounded a whistle alarm and the entire settlement evacuated to a blockhouse.

The Northern Indians landed and set up a camp at the edge of the settlement. They were still camped there when the *Massachusetts* arrived on November 20. The captain of the gunboat, Samuel Swartwout, sent eighteen armed soldiers and an interpreter to "have a friendly talk" with the intruders. His offer was that they not only leave immediately, but that he would make sure they left by towing them in their canoes over to Victoria.

The Northern Indians ridiculed the offer and threatened the officers, daring them to fight. The men returned to the ship and reported to the captain.

According to Swartwout's ship's log, he sent forty-five men out again into a rainy afternoon, carrying a flag of truce. They repeated his offer, and the Northern Indians were even more "menacing and insulting" than before. The men once again returned to ship. At 6 p.m., Swartwout moved the *Massachusetts* to within 600 yards of the camp, just offshore.

He used the services of a smaller civilian steamer, the *Traveler*, to make his next move. When darkness fell, they readied the *Traveler* with a small cannon and a howitzer. They kept watch all night to keep the Indians from sneaking away. Early the next morning, thirty-nine men formed a landing party, which waded through the heavy surf with the howitzer. They took up position on the beach. The interpreter told the Indians this was their last warning, pointing at the howitzer and the cannon aimed at their camp. The Indians again rebuffed them.

Accounts are inconsistent as to who began firing first, but the battle began in earnest. The navy fired grapeshot (clumps of small iron balls) and round shot (large cannon balls) into the camp and surrounding woods where the Indians had taken cover. After the bombardment scattered the Indians, the sailors charged into the camp, setting fire to everything, including their canoes.

The battle lasted a little over three hours. One sailor, Gustav Engelbrecht, was shot in the head and killed by an Indian's bullet. The American sailors counted twenty-seven Indians dead and a good number of wounded.

By the end of the afternoon, with the camp destroyed and the surviving Indians hiding in the dense forest, the navy sent a captured woman in to tell them to surrender under the original terms. The Indians responded that they would fight to the death. However, by the next day, they had changed their minds. Their two remaining chiefs surrendered unconditionally. One other chief had been killed. Of 117 warriors, twenty-seven were dead and twenty-one were wounded.

The ship's log records that eighty-six Indians were escorted onto the *Massachusetts* as prisoners of war. There had been ninety-six American sailors involved.

They left Port Gamble on November 24 and sailed for Esquimalt, arriving the next day. There, Swartwout and Vancouver Island's Governor Douglas had a disagreement about what to do with the prisoners. Swartwout wanted to leave them there, but Douglas wanted nothing to do with them.

Finally, Swartwout agreed to take them further north. Newspaper reports said he purchased canoes, blankets, and food, and took them up the eastern shore of Vancouver Island, letting them off 25 miles north of Nanaimo. The Indians promised they would never come back.

Swartwout returned to Puget Sound and passed these assurances on to his fellow Americans, many of whom were skeptical. Sure enough, several weeks later, a group of sixty or so Northern Indians landed on San Juan Island. They told a Hudson Bay agent that, because they had lost a *tyee*, or chief, at Port Gamble, they intended to kill a U.S. customs inspector, Oscar Olney, who was considered a chief. They also said they intended to take "five Boston heads" home with them. The agent warned Oscar Olney about the threat, after which he hurried off to the relative safety of Port Townsend.

A few months earlier, another local "Boston" had moved his family from Port Townsend back to Whidbey Island. Isaac Ebey and his wife, Emily, had three children—two little boys, Eason and Ellison, and Emily's daughter by her first marriage, Anna Sconce. They ran a small farmstead on Whidbey Island, which they called "The Cabins." Like Oscar Olney, Isaac Ebey was a U.S. customs official. His parents and one or two brothers also lived on Whidbey Island. The Ebeys had, of course, heard of all the troubles with the Northern Indians, but that did not let that stop them from going on with their lives.

In April 1857, about five months after the events at Port Gamble, a group of Northern Indians made a nighttime landing at Whatcom. They ransacked a settler's cabin and chased him out. They let it be known that they intended to take the heads of several Bostons who were leaders at Fort Bellingham, including Colonel Edmund Fitzhugh, Captain Pickett, and Russell V. Peabody. After this, residents organized a volunteer company to stand guard at Fort Bellingham.

Meanwhile, Oscar Olney received word from Governor James Douglas of Vancouver Island that he was still in danger because 300 Northern Indians had arrived at Victoria and another 300 at Nanaimo. The USS *Massachusetts* was no longer in the Sound, having headed back to San Francisco. People were worried. On Whidbey Island, some settlers left. The Ebeys stayed.

At the end of April, a schooner called the *Phantom* was *en route* from Port Townsend to Victoria when a group of Northern Indians boarded and robbed them. Another schooner, the HC *Page*, arrived in Olympia saying they had been chased by a very large canoe of sixty men and that they had seen three or four other canoes in the area. At Apple Tree Cove, on May 7, Northern Indians attacked and killed several S'Klallams, though newspapers provided no further details.

On May 25, twelve canoes carrying Northern Indians arrived at Ebey's Landing on Whidbey Island. They flew white flags and asked residents for water, which was given to them. They left.

On a hot afternoon on August 11, a small group of Northern Indians came to "The Cabins" and asked Ebey if they could buy some flour and sugar. He told them "no." As they left, they stopped to speak to a young workman, Thomas Hastie, who was cradling oats. They asked him about the number of people living there and if Ebey was a chief.

That night, the family dog, Rover, woke up the household with his barking. Isaac Ebey got up and went outside. Emily Ebey was right behind her husband, along with others from the household. Isaac stopped suddenly and spoke into the darkness, where an unknown number of Indians was gathered. He asked them what they wanted. They said something in English, but Emily could not understand. She heard two shots. She and the others rushed back into the house and into another room, crowding at a window to try and see what was happening. Emily saw Isaac outside the window and called to him to get back inside the house. He did not respond but staggered around holding his head, then lurched away into the night. She heard two more shots and banging at the front door.

Emily Ebey, her three children, and two houseguests, Mr. and Mrs. Corliss, escaped out the window as the Indians entered the house through the front door. They ran into the forest to the sound of crashing and pottery breaking behind them. Mrs. Corliss and Eason Ebey were separated from the group and made their escape by climbing over a fence. Someone shot at them and Mrs. Corliss felt a ball passing by near her face. They kept running until they came to a neighbor's home and banged on the door. It was 2 a.m.

When they heard what happened, the men in the house got their guns and went back to the Ebey place. There were no signs of Indians. In the front yard, they found the bloodied, headless corpse of Isaac Ebey.

After going through the house, they sent word to Isaac's brother, Winfield Ebey, and his parents, Jacob and Sarah Ebey. The neighbors prevailed on them to wait until morning before going over to the house. Winfield described the scene in his diary:

> His Headless trunk lay on its side near the end of the porch apparently where he had fallen. When I knelt by his side & took his rigid hands in mine there was no room for doubt as to identity. Although the head was not there I Could have recognized him among a thousand. I have seen death often before & have seen the bodies of persons Killd by savages but I never yet saw so horrible a sight as this. I never before saw the Human head severed from the body.[1]

They carried Isaac's body into the house, which was in a shambles. They shouted into the woods for the other survivors and finally heard a response from Mr. Corliss. They found the whole party in the woods, wet and shivering from a terror-filled night in the elements.

More neighbors arrived. They washed and laid out Isaac's body. He had been shot with a ball and two buck shot in the right side. The ball had passed entirely through the body, breaking his left arm. Another buckshot had blasted off a finger. A neighbor made a coffin and they dug a grave next to Isaac's first wife, Rebecca.

Isaac Ebey was a prominent citizen and the news of his murder spread quickly. Authorities located and arrested a group of seven Northern Indians. The arrests continued until they had a total of eighteen people in irons.

The entire region went under high alert and angry citizens threatened to grab the prisoners and hang them all. The Ebey family packed up what was left in their ransacked home and moved into a blockhouse near Jacob and Sarah Ebey's place.

Recriminations spread—why did the Ebeys not have any firearms in the home? Why did Thomas Hastie, the worker, not warn the family the Indians had been asking if a chief lived there?

In the end, officials were never able to discover conclusively who murdered Isaac Ebey. The most specific information came from Governor Douglas of Victoria, who said the killers were from Kuiu Island in "Russian America" (Alaska). Known today for having the highest population of black bears in the world—three to five per square mile—Kuiu Island was home to a village of Kuiu Kwan Tlingit people in Tebenkof Bay.

Douglas said the information had come from Fort Simpson, where a reporting party had seen the murderers go by with the head of Isaac Ebey. He said the leader of the attack party was the brother of a chief killed by the USS *Massachusetts* at Port Gamble.

Several years later, a steamer captain named Dodd purchased Isaac Ebey's scalp from a group of Northern Indians. He passed it on to Mr. A. M. Poe, a friend of Isaac's, who gave it to Winfield Ebey. Winfield wrote in his diary that his brother's scalp still had all the hair and ears.

In March 1862, a ship arrived in Victoria from San Francisco. One of the passengers had smallpox. The disease spread quickly although most whites were able to get vaccinated and survived what became a devastating epidemic. Most Indians were not given vaccinations and had no immunity. Within a year, about half of the Northern Indians were dead of smallpox, including 60 percent of the Tlingit and 70 percent of the Haida. The village of Tlingit people on Kuiu Island was wiped out.

3

The Murder of Chief Swell (1861)

On a late February day in 1861, a large Makah canoe set out from Port Townsend headed for Neah Bay. Three men, four women, and a boy occupied the canoe. They carried 1,000 dollars' worth of goods, including potware, blankets, and a dozen yards of calico, plus two months' worth of mail. Much of this was the property of the Bostons.

In charge of the expedition was a young Makah chief named Wha-laltl Asabuy. Due to his penchant for wearing a fine Boston suit and the proud way he carried himself, the Bostons called him "Swell."

They made their way west along the northern shore of the Olympic Peninsula, stopping at Dungeness to pick up a load of potatoes, a favorite among the Makah. By the time they left Dungeness, it was 7 p.m. and dark.

After rowing for some hours, they spotted a campfire at Crescent Bay and headed in. As they landed through heavy surf, they discovered too late that the camp was a group of Elwha that included an enemy of Swell's known as Met-so-nack, also known in English as Elwha Charley. Hastily, Swell and the others shoved the canoe back into the water, but it was too late. Elwha Charley pulled out a gun and shot Swell in the back, killing him instantly.

The Makah dragged Swell into the canoe and tried to escape but the canoe was too heavy and the surf too rough. They abandoned the canoe and swam away. They all made it to shore, escaping silently into the woods, while the canoe broke up against the rocks. It took the survivors three days to make their way home to Neah Bay.

Word of Swell's murder soon reached Port Townsend and Swell's friend, James G. Swan. A white man, Swan had organized the expedition with Swell, and some of its contents were his property.

Swell was one of the Makah chiefs who had signed the 1855 Treaty of Neah Bay. He was well-known for his intelligence and prowess as a canoeman. Due to his "posh sartorial preferences," he enjoyed the nickname the Bostons had given him. He was popular among the Bostons, having garnered their attention when he rescued the crew of the brig *Swiss Boy* in 1859, when it wrecked in Barclay Sound on Vancouver Island. The brig's crew had been captured by a group of Ohiet and Sheshat, who considered anything beached on their land to be theirs, including slaves. Swell had helped to convince them to let the crew go. This act was the beginning of a mutually beneficial relationship and though Swell was young, the Bostons considered him an important Makah ally.

James Swan, known today for his historical journals, had befriended Swell a year and half earlier, and the two had developed a close relationship. Swan had lived with the Makah at Neah Bay and was popular there for his artistic skills. He had stuck to a policy when dealing with the Makah that served him well—to always be civil, never lie, and do not go around flashing weapons.

He and Swell called themselves "winter brothers." They often swapped favors and taught each other the ways of their people. Swan painted a horse and Swell's name on the sail for the latter's canoe. When Swan learned of Swell's death, he was shattered and angry, and he knew there would be more trouble.

Meanwhile, the morning after the shooting, the Elwha camping at Crescent Bay discovered the goods floating in the surf along with the wreckage from Swell's canoe. They gathered what they could but most of it was ruined. They realized at that point that the items likely belonged to whites. This worried them enough that several of the Elwha approached some local white men and led them to the ruined shipment. They also pulled Swell's body out of the water and wrapped it in blankets. One of the white men, Captain Thompson, made a box for the body and readied it for shipment to Neah Bay.

James Swan set out from Port Townsend on March 7 with a group of S'Klallams, including their chief, Cheech-Ma-Ham, also known as Chetzemoka, or the "Duke of York." Along the way, they stopped at Dungeness, Yennis (possibly Ennis Creek), and Chewitsen (located at today's Port Angeles), trying to get more information about what happened.

Bad weather made the journey by water difficult and they left their canoes 4 or 5 miles away and walked to the Elwha village at the mouth of the Elwha River. When they arrived, Chetzemoka served as interpreter, telling the Elwha that the Bostons wanted their property back and wanted Swell's body. Swan wrote about the meeting in his journals:

> Charley, the murderer, then got up and made a speech. He said that he shot Swell for two reasons, one of which was, that the Mackahs had killed two of the Elwha's a few months previous, and they were determined to kill a Mackah chief to pay for it. And the other reason was, that Swell had

taken his squaw away, and would not return either the woman or the fifty blankets he had paid for her.[1]

Charley assured the visitors that he was very sorry there were white men's goods in the canoe. Around seventy-five Elwha were present for this encounter, and it is likely they were not very happy with Charley for creating this problem for the tribe. They asked Swan's advice for the best course of action, wanting his help in fending off a possible revenge attack from the Makah and their allies, the Nittinat. Swan promised he would explain what happened to the Indian agent and induce him to handle the matter. He said he would convince the Makah not to take action but to let the agent resolve the issue.

Swan later wrote that he was very angry during this meeting but held his tongue. He wanted to hang Elwha Charley on the spot, but these feelings were allayed by the fact that the other Elwha were asking his advice. He gathered up what was left of the goods from the canoe, along with Swell's body, and went back to Port Townsend.

Within the week, two of Swell's brothers and several Makah arrived in Port Townsend from Neah Bay. Together with Swan, they paddled south through the Sound to the Puyallup Reservation where Col. Simmons, the Indian agent, was located. Simmons had recently been removed from his position but had not yet been replaced. Like Swan, he was a friend of Swell's, and he was angry about the murder. Swan wrote a long letter about the incident, which was published in the *Washington Standard*:

> This outrage was one that the department, as well as the citizens, felt bound to see redressed. Swell was too good an Indian, and too valuable a man both to the department and the white settlers, to have this murder go unavenged. The many acts of kindness he has done the white men, the shipwrecked mariners he has relieved, and the peculiar tact he had in imparting the information of the whites to his tribe, made him a person of the first importance, particularly in the coming of the payment of the annuities.[2]

Unfortunately, Simmons said he did not have the funds to take any action. He was understaffed and was still waiting for the arrival of the tribe's annuities, due under the 1855 treaty. He could not pay for someone to hunt down and arrest Elwha Charley or do anything else about the murder. However, he promised that as soon as he could, he would take action.

Swan agreed to take Swell's body back to Neah Bay and try to convince the Makah to leave the matter to the agents. He was even angrier than before, and his letter to the *Washington Standard* decried the neglect and inaction of the Indian agency.

When Swan arrived back in Neah Bay with Swell's body, Swell's brother Peter asked Swan to help him select a good spot to bury Swell. Peter also asked Swan to repaint Swell's Tomanawos board, a cedar plaque that was said to have magical qualities related to the deceased.

Six months passed, and nothing was done about the murder of Chief Swell. The Indian agent, Simmons, was gone, replaced by Mr. Webster, who ran a trading post in the Neah Bay area. Although much of the lost merchandise had been his, Webster took no action.

The Makah lost patience. Led by an old war chief, Cowbetsi, and Swell's brother Peter, they declared that Simmons had lied to them and that they would "go ourselves and kill the Elwhas." On November 2, 1861, James Swan watched while a Makah war party of 80 men prepared for a revenge expedition. The men painted their bodies black and tied their hair into club knots on top of their heads, bound with fir twigs. They decorated their canoes with fir boughs. Most of the men had firearms; others carried bows and arrows, spears, and knives. They made torches using 5-foot poles, faggots, and pitch-wood, declaring that they were going to burn the Elwha village, kill as many as they could, and take slaves.

Swan happened to know that most of the Elwhas were not actually in their villages, having travelled to the reservation at the head of the Hood Canal to pick up their annuities. It is not clear whether he told the Makahs that or not.

Webster tried to talk them out of going, but they did not listen. As the war party set off from Neah Bay in twelve canoes, they whooped and yelled, firing guns and singing war songs. The women and elders climbed up on their roofs and beat them with sticks, shrieking their support. Swan later wrote what happened next:

> The war party lucked upon a hapless pair of Elwhas hunting seals at Crescent Bay, the precise site of Swell's murder. When blood was most ready to answer blood, the two were simply targets of opportunity. Having shot and beheaded them, the Makahs noted the alarms being shrieked by several Elwha women who had watched the ambush from a distance, held a rapid council, and decided revenge had been sufficiently done.[3]

Three days later, the canoes returned, the men shooting muskets and shouting songs of victory. They brought with them the heads of the two Elwhas they had killed. They put the heads on stakes and set the stakes in the sand on the beach, forming a song circle around their trophies. They called upon Swan to enter the circle and stand next to the gruesome prizes while Chief Cowbetsi made a speech. The chief said that they had killed the two Elwhas because the Indian agent had failed to take any action over the murder of Chief Swell.

They asked Swan if he knew who the heads belonged to. He knew one of them, Tire-buch-ton, who was one of the Elwhas who had helped kill Swell, but he didn't know who the other was. Cowbetsi told him, "'That is Tsa-why-ark,' said he, 'and now I want to talk to you.'"[4]

He complained that Simmons had not done what he said he would do and had made fools of the Makah. Swan replied that Simmons had been a good friend of Swell's, as he himself was, but that he had been relieved and therefore could do nothing. He reminded them that Webster was their friend and that the latter had not wanted them to go and take revenge.

Cowbetsi told him that they had not killed anyone else, did not take any women for slaves, and had not burned a village because they did not want to upset Webster.

Many Makahs felt that the score had been settled at that point, although it's not clear whether the Elwha saw it that way. Swell's brother Peter, years later, asked an Elwha chief to kill Charley, but it appears that only the two beheaded Elwhas paid for the murder. It is unknown what happened to the woman that Swell reportedly had stolen.

4

A Most Hardened Character (1877)

One spring morning in 1878, Port Townsend's jailer climbed down through the trap door that led into the basement of the jailhouse. This is where his four current prisoners lived in cramped cells with small, heavily barred windows. To his shock and embarrassment, he found the basement and its cells empty.

As word got out, an outcry arose across town, but not all of it carried a tone of outrage. One of the escaped prisoners was Henry L. Sutton, a former newspaperman in town. Henry had friends, good friends. It was in his cell that deputies found the means of escape—a saw and a chisel—which he had used to cut a hole in the floor and dig a tunnel.

During the day, Henry had apparently covered the hole with a nice little rug that one of his comrades had provided, along with the tools. He also had a small donated table that he kept over the rug. He had decorated his cell with other niceties as well, including flowers, books, and tasty goodies. The other prisoners, less popular than Henry, had obviously followed him out. More than one of the prisoners was in jail for murder, and that included Henry.

Henry was an articulate, attractive, and literate man who had come from humble beginnings. He was born around 1835 and raised in the Lower East Side of Manhattan. Port Townsend's early historian, James McCurdy, described Henry as coming from "Boston shipping people," but that may have been an appealing story that Henry himself manufactured. In fact, his father was a shipmaster, or sea captain, but not a shipping magnate as implied by "Boston shipping people." His mother was the daughter of a local butcher.

Edmond Day Sutton, Henry's father, died around 1842, when Henry was seven. His mother, Ann, henceforth lived with her four children at 9 Rivington Street, in the Lower East Side's Bowery. This period marked the beginning of the area's transformation into the notorious slum crowded with tenement houses where immigrants were packed by the dozens into small apartments meant for single families.

The census of 1850 shows Ann Sutton as head of a household, along with her four children and eight other residents, or "inmates" as household members were called.

Henry apparently left home for California that year at the age of fifteen, a year after the California gold rush began. He probably tried his hand at gold mining but quickly switched to the lucrative business of selling provisions to miners.

In 1857, twenty years before his Port Townsend jail escape, twenty-two-year-old Henry returned to the east coast, where he soon got tangled up in his first known killing. The episode occurred in Boston, where Henry was visiting his brother George, a mariner, whom he likely had not seen in years. The brothers were carousing down by the wharves with a third man, Sylvester L. Bacon, master of the schooner *Galota*.

As they walked along the street, Sylvester Bacon entered the yard of a boarding house. There, he engaged in what was variously described as "unseemly acts," an act of "grossness," and "answering a call of nature."

Unfortunately, his unseemly act was viewed by a group of ladies and gentlemen inside the front room of the boarding house, and it caused a great deal of consternation. The owner, Margaret Fagan, directed two of her boarders, John Donovan and Michael Kelly, to go deal with the situation. Kelly headed off to find a policeman while Donovan confronted the lads outside.

Newspaper accounts differ as to who attacked whom first, but they all agree that a violent physical altercation ensued. Donovan quickly found himself overpowered and he escaped back into the house. Meanwhile, Kelly returned, not with a policeman but with a neighbor named John Hilton, also known as "Limerick Boy," a locally celebrated pugilist.

Limerick Boy engaged the three men in battle and Donovan came back out to help. He tangled with Henry Sutton, who suddenly pulled out a long-bladed knife called a dirk, and stabbed Donovan. He kept stabbing, plunging the dirk into Donovan's arm, shoulder, head, and breast. When Donovan went down, Henry jumped away. Somehow, Donovan was still alive, and he dragged himself back into the house.

As officers arrived, the three intruders took off running, Limerick Boy hot on their heels. He soon caught up with Henry, who turned to fight. Limerick Boy broke a cane over Henry's head and Henry stabbed him in the neck so deep it sliced into his lungs. Others arrived and wrestled the dirk out of Henry's hands, but not before he managed to stab another man, Jacob Todd, in the thigh.

Police hauled Henry off to jail. George Sutton and Sylvester Bacon had escaped and were hurrying back to their respective ships, but police intercepted and arrested both. Meanwhile, both John Donovan and John Hilton, a.k.a. Limerick Boy, died of their knife wounds.

Henry insisted to his jailers that he had killed the men in self-defense, that he was not intoxicated, and that he only carried a dirk out of habit after living in the treacherous wilds of California. He claimed that Donovan attacked him first, and that Limerick Boy had also brandished a knife and stabbed him in the leg. This was corroborated when Henry showed a leg injury.

Henry was reportedly distressed when he learned that the men had both died. He apparently made a good case for himself—when he was tried on manslaughter charges, the jury found him not guilty.

He was soon back on the West Coast, and by 1858 or so, he was living in Port Townsend, Washington Territory. There, from 1860 to 1861, he served briefly as editor of the *Port Townsend Register*. In the late 1860s, he became the editor and publisher of a new newspaper, *The Message*, during which he reportedly developed a reputation as a "fearless and capable" editor (per McCurdy). This paper went belly up in the early 1870s.

Although Henry was clearly intelligent and resourceful, he was also bedeviled by money and alcohol problems, not to mention a nature that was unusually violent, even for violent times. Over the next few years, he was a defendant in over half a dozen court cases, mostly involving unpaid debts. He faced a foreclosure and was charged for damaging someone's property.

In 1872, he was involved in a fracas during which his dinner companion knifed a drunken man to death after the man badgered them during their meal and then pulled a knife. Despite witness testimony during the inquest, which described Henry's friend stabbing the man after the man slashed him in the face, the district attorney charged both Henry and his friend with murder. He later dropped Henry from the charge sheet and Henry's friend was acquitted by a jury.

November of 1875 found Henry "fitting up the old ware-house on the Union wharf for a saloon," known as the Blue Light.[1] The Blue Light was a thriving business, serving alcohol to thirsty mariners, plus fish and oysters every day for lunch.

This state of affairs came to a crashing end in May 1877. On that spring afternoon, a boat pilot from England named Charles Howard walked down Tibbal's wharf with another man. Howard had reportedly once been a friend of Henry's, but they had fallen out. Some said the hostility was over a girl, but there had also been a recent altercation having to do with a dog.

Charles himself had a bad reputation in some quarters and had been charged twice with attempted murder, cases that were apparently dropped. At least one acquaintance described him as a valiant pilot who had saved his little schooner, the *Winifred*, and its passengers when they hit a horrific storm off the coast at Port Angeles. According to this passenger, Howard had engaged in a heroic two-hour battle against an angry sea to maneuver the *Winifred* to safety inside the Port Angeles harbor. The man said that "[n]o word was spoken during those two hours but the orders of Captain Howard and the aye, aye, sir, of the man at the fore sheet."[2]

On this day, Charles's companion entered the Blue Light to speak to someone, while Charles lingered near the door, unwilling to enter. At that moment, a boy walked into the saloon to deliver Henry's supper. As Henry began to eat, he noticed Charles. The two men exchanged words. Charles called the Blue Light a "bawdy house" and Henry was a "low-lived, black-hearted son of a b—h."

Henry abandoned his meal, declaring, "No d—d man ever called me that and lived." He grabbed his "English dragoon, self-cocking, four-barreled revolver," sprang forward and fired.[3] Charles drew his revolver, but before he could fire, he took a bullet in the abdomen. As Charles went down, Henry fired again, striking him in the shoulder. Henry fired twice more but missed.

After two bystanders carried a moaning Charles away from the saloon, Henry announced that he would go get his "old girl." He produced a "breach-loading sixteen-shooter rifle, plus a double-barreled shotgun."[4] He loaded all his weapons and waited behind the bar.

A former sheriff then came into the saloon and quietly took a position near the door. Henry swore at him and said, "I have a good mind to kill you. I've killed one of your crowd, you are another, and there are ten or twenty more, and I'll kill you all and done with it."[5]

The man stepped quietly back out of the saloon. Henry set his pile of weapons on the bar and announced, "The first man that ventures near me I'll blow him through." Then he finished eating.

Some minutes ticked by. Presently, a friend of Henry's named Fred Pontefract came into the Blue Light and suggested that Henry might want to get out of there. Henry proclaimed he would stay and fight, but Fred finally persuaded him to leave. Forty-five minutes had passed since Henry shot Charles Howard when Henry walked out of the saloon with his weapons, $2,000 in coin, and a few other personal items.

As he and Fred headed through the crowds on the wharf, he invited the "boys" to go into the saloon and drink whatever they wanted. "I've no use for what's there anymore," he said. "I'm going away for a while."[6] He and Fred picked out a boat that looked suitable and climbed in. No one made a move to stop them. They rowed out into the harbor and into the Strait of Juan de Fuca.

Once Henry had safely escaped, the indignant citizenry roared and demanded his arrest. However, the sheriff of Port Townsend, Sheriff Miller, was away on business in Steilacoom so nothing was done. Upon his return, Sheriff Miller formed a posse and they set out to hunt down the fugitives.

Meanwhile, the two men had rowed out to a steamer, which took them and their stolen boat to the lighthouse on the Port Angeles spit. There, the fugitives spent the night, inexplicably describing their plans to the lighthouse keeper.

The next day, they were still at the lighthouse when the mail boat came by. Henry hailed it and asked the mail man if he had any news from Port Townsend. The mail man told him that Charles had died of his gunshot wound. The mail man later reported that Henry appeared to be shaken at the news.

After getting the bad news about Charles, Henry hired a man to take the stolen boat back to its owner in Port Townsend. He and Fred walked off into the woods, headed for a friend's cabin in Freshwater Bay at the mouth of the Elwha.

Unfortunately for them, they soon became lost. They spent several days deep in the woods, floundering amongst the sword ferns, bogs, and fallen logs. Eventually, they gave up hope of getting out of there alive. In desperation, they discarded their loads, which may or may not have included the $2,000 in gold coin that Henry had brought with him.

Amazingly, the two men found their way out. They came upon the beach at Freshwater Bay and the friend's cabin. They ate a good meal, grateful for their escape, and fell into bed.

Meanwhile, Sheriff Miller learned from the lighthouse keeper where the fugitives were headed, and he and his posse headed straight to Freshwater Bay. That night, the posse surrounded the cabin. When the men inside were all fast asleep, the posse entered and made the arrests without incident.[7]

Four months later, Henry went on trial. On September 13, 1877, the jury found him guilty of manslaughter and sentenced him to five years. Fred was let go.

Washington Territory had no penitentiary so they jailed Henry in Port Townsend. During his first six months there, he planned his escape, secretly cutting a hole into the floor of his cell and digging a tunnel.

Within a week or two after the four men had escaped, word arrived in town that Oregon lawmen had captured three of them near Astoria. The three did not include Henry Sutton.

Over the years, rumors put Henry in Mexico or killed in a shoot-out in Arizona. Henry Sutton was never apprehended, and his fate remains a mystery.

As a young boy growing up in Port Townsend, local historian James McCurdy and his brothers spent many fine afternoons searching for Henry Sutton's gold. A great deal of speculation developed over the years about the $2,000 in gold coin that Henry took with him that fateful day when he left the Blue Light saloon, and the legend grew apace with the speculation. A favorite story was that he had stashed it in an orchard owned by a man named Benn Pettygrove. Others said it must be somewhere along the numerous logging roads around the town.

What the lads did not know was that perhaps a better place to search for the treasure was not the woods around Port Townsend, but the woods around Port Angeles and Freshwater Bay, where Henry Sutton and Fred Pontefract were forced to discard their heavy loads in a desperate attempt to survive.

5

The Trial of Xwelas, "The Old Woman" (1878)

On Christmas Day in 1878, a pregnant Orcas Island woman named Xwelas (Hwe-LASS) crouched in the bushes. A baby strapped to her back, she waited in silence for her husband, George, to come up the path through the trees. Her face was smeared with blood from injuries George had given her after he got drunk at a neighbor's Christmas party the night before. After she spent the night in a woodshed with her baby, he had told her to pack her things and get out. Now, she clutched a shotgun, loaded and ready.

Exactly what happened next was unclear. George Phillips appeared on the path, walking with Xwelas's teenage son from an earlier marriage, Mason Fitzhugh. The gun exploded and George lurched to the ground, his body riddled with buckshot. He called to his stepson to save him as he expired, telling him, "You're the only friend I've got!" Mason Fitzhugh took the gun away from his mother and ran off to get help.

He found a neighbor, James Tulloch, and begged him to help move George before the hogs could get at him. Tulloch asked him who shot George and Mason replied, "the old woman." Xwelas, also known as Mary Phillips, was quickly arrested for murder and taken to the jail in Port Townsend. Although everyone knew that George beat her often, no one, perhaps not even Xwelas herself, assumed she would escape the hangman's noose.

Xwelas was born in the 1830s to a Salish chief. Originally of the S'Klallam tribe, her people were related to the Lummi and Samish people and ended up in the Bellingham area. Her father was Skwa-Skway, Chief Sehome, and her mother was Cha-tu-sia-Skwa-Skwa, Princess Sehome. Her brother, S'ya-whom (anglicized to Sehome), became a Samish chief after his father. The neighborhood of Sehome in Bellingham was named for him by the white man who platted the area, Edmund Clare Fitzhugh.

This was a period when whites and indigenous people mixed readily, primarily due to trade. White women were a rarity and white frontiersmen often married into local tribes. The connection between the family of Xwelas and white settlers began with the marriage of the aforementioned Edmund Clare Fitzhugh and Xwelas's niece, Julie, the daughter of Sehome.

Fitzhugh was one of the most prominent citizens in the region. Originally from Virginia, he served there in the legislature, then became an attorney in California during the 1840s. He headed north to the Pacific Northwest in the 1850s and was one of the earliest white settlers in the region. He had been involved in the famed Pig War of 1859, at the end of which the United States claimed possession of the San Juans from Britain.

Fitzhugh held numerous titles during his time in the Pacific Northwest, including Indian agent, county auditor, customs inspector, and aide to Governor Isaac Stevens. U.S. President Buchanan appointed him a United States judge for Washington Territory, a position he held for four years. By both the white settlers and the local tribes, he was considered a leading citizen, or *tyee* (chief). This status helped him negotiate a marriage for himself with the sixteen-year-old daughter of Chief Sehome, E-yow-alth, whom he called Julie. He was twenty years older than her.

About a year after his marriage to "Julie," the teenager's unmarried aunt, Xwelas, came to visit the couple at their home on Bellingham Bay. Julie was already busy caring for her new baby daughter, Julia. It is unknown how the relationship developed, but eventually, Edmund Fitzhugh indulged in a local custom normally enjoyed only by Native American men—he took a second wife. Xwelas, who was in her twenties, moved in with the couple as wife number two.

Perhaps because of his relatively high status and the scarcity of disapproving white women, Fitzhugh's polygamous marriage did not seem to raise eyebrows amongst the whites. If it did, the *tsking* did not make it into the local papers. However, Fitzhugh did possess certain questionable personality traits. He shot and killed another man over a gambling debt in 1858. Due to his lofty position as federal judge, he reportedly had a hand in acquitting himself of this crime.

It is unknown whether the household was a happy one, but Xwelas, whom he renamed Mary, eventually bore him two sons—Mason and Julius. However, after several years of this arrangement, Fitzhugh decided it did not quite suit him. He packed up his eldest child, his daughter Julia, and took off for Seattle, abandoning both of his wives.

The fate of young Julia is unknown, though her mother later remarried another man. The Civil War found Fitzhugh back in the east, fighting on the side of the Confederacy. He survived that experience and went on to form another family somewhere in the South. As he had done with his Salish family in Bellingham, he abandoned them. Still not finished with this routine, he went on to form yet a third family in Iowa, whom he also abandoned.

In the 1870s, Fitzhugh returned to the Seattle area and tried to establish relations with his son, Mason (one of Xwelas's sons), but Mason had stayed with his mother and wanted nothing to do with his capricious father. In 1883, Edmund Fitzhugh was found degenerated and quite dead in a San Francisco hotel room.

Meanwhile, having been abandoned, E-yow-alth, or Julie, now childless, remarried to another white man. Xwelas also married another white man, this one an immigrant from Florida called William King Lear. Ancestry records indicate that as a military officer, William had married the daughter of Chief Chenoweth of the Cascade tribe in the Columbia River region. This marriage lasted a couple years before he was transferred. His wife refused to leave her people, so he went alone. He later migrated to the north and married Xwelas, who was now in her thirties. Around 1866, she gave birth to her third son, Billy King Lear.

William worked as a land speculator and ran a store and enjoyed some status in the white settlement. Shortly after that, William became the second of Xwelas's husbands to abandon her and the children. He reportedly went back to Florida for a time, then ended up in Alaska in his later years. He died in 1915, a patient at Western State Hospital, and is buried there.

Xwelas, in her early forties now, had three sons, no husband, and no means of support other than the communal generosity of her family and tribe. Having been abandoned twice by men who were likely considered a good match at the time, her third and last husband was a step down. George Phillips was a laborer with a bad reputation. From Wales, he worked as a cooper at the Langdon Lime Works on Orcas Island. On February 9, 1873, Xwelas married George and became Mrs. Mary Phillips.

George was known as a violent drunkard with a bad temper. Neighbors testified at her trial that he beat her regularly and that she fought back ferociously.

Xwelas bore George several children. The name of the oldest two (or perhaps only one) are unknown and the family was struck by tragedy in 1877. The four-year-olds (by some accounts, one male toddler) were playing at the lime works where George worked. The children dropped a lighted match into a powder keg, which exploded, killing them instantly. A year later, at the time of George's death, Xwelas had a baby girl named Maggie and was pregnant again.

Press reports about the shooting were scant and unsympathetic. The *Times-Colonist* in Victoria seemed to find the incident amusing and accused the *kloochman* (Chinook jargon for an indigenous woman) of shooting her husband out of a fit of jealousy when he flirted with another woman. The article about the shooting did not say the couple were married, but that the victim "had been living with a *kloochman* for a few years." The editors did not bother to name Xwelas, but variously refer to her as "the *kloochman*," "squaw," or "maiden of the forest." The article also claimed that Xwelas tried to shoot her own son, Mason Fitzhugh, but that he escaped.[1]

Mason's testimony at the trial said nothing about his mother trying to shoot him. He described what he had witnessed, which was that his stepfather had suddenly been shot and that he saw his mother standing by the bushes with the shotgun.

Testifying in her own defense, Xwelas told the court that the night before, on Christmas Eve, she and George had gone to a party at the house of a white neighbor, William Shattuck. There was a lot of drinking and gambling. She said that George had gotten very drunk and became belligerent during their journey home:

After we had gone some distance George said, "where were you last night, you old whore you, when I was hunting for you?" After some quarreling I called him a dog & he struck me with the oar on the cheek, then everything became dark and I fell forward. I then rose up & picked up the child when he punched me in the side with the oar. I then called him a dog & said, "don't you know I've got a child in my bowels?" He said he didn't care if he killed me; he'd get another woman, that I was whoring with Siwashes.

When I recovered from the blow I resolved to pay him back and asked him for the paddle to steer with, when he gave me it, I struck him twice with it, once on the face and once on the shoulder.[2]

She continued to testify, saying he repeatedly threatened to kill her after they got home. "George told me to get my things and leave, calling me a slut. He demanded the key to the house & ere I could give it to him, he took the axe & broke open the door."[3]

George then grabbed two guns and began loading them. Her son, Mason, tried to reason with her that George would sober up, trying to get her to stay, but she decided to spend the night in the woods with her baby, Maggie. She took a double-barreled shotgun and left the house, sleeping in a neighbor's root cellar. In the morning, she saw George and Mason walking along the trail, so she hid in the bushes. Yet Maggie cried out "Papa."

I raised up from behind the brush. George then rushed forward & grasped the gun by the middle of the barrel. We each tried to pull the gun from the other, & while we were thus struggling the gun went off shooting George. He staggered back calling for Mason … Mason came and said to me, "Do you see what you have done?" I answered, "I see what I have done."[4]

Despite her claims of an accidental shooting, evidence showed that buckshot from her shotgun had ripped up the foliage alongside the path where she had been standing. This indicated that she had shot from behind the bushes, not at close quarters during a struggle. Also, George's body had no powder burns on it.

However, numerous witnesses testified that Xwelas was afraid for her life, that George threatened her and beat her. She told Mason right after the shooting that she did it because George was going to kill her. One witness was the notorious Colonel Enoch May, who was not a real colonel but a smuggler of opium and Chinese laborers from Vancouver Island, all-around crooked politician, erstwhile reporter, and fraudster. He was also a trafficker of Indian brides to white men, supplying women for a fee. May was present at the party that precipitated the shooting and testified about George's drinking and temper.

Another witness was James Francis Tulloch, also a key figure in the history of Orcas Island. He was a religious man of great piety, who hoped to remove the native population and settle Orcas Island with whites only. He did not approve of "half breed" children being produced by the unions between native women and white men and campaigned vigorously against miscegenation. He also railed against the Chinese and other non-white races.

Several witnesses supported an insanity defense, testifying that Xwelas was crazy and that she had not been in her right mind since the death of her children at the lime kiln. One person testified that Xwelas believed that the explosion had been a plot of some sort. Another claimed that George repeatedly declared that his wife was crazy. Mason also testified that his mother was sometimes not in her right mind. It is not clear whether Mason really believed that or if he was just trying to save his mother from being hanged for murder.

After a two-day trial, the jury went out. They soon found her guilty of manslaughter but not of murder. The presiding judge, Roger Greene, gave her a relatively light sentence of two years, minus the ten months she had already spent in prison. During the period of her incarceration, she bore her last child.

The 1880 census shows Mary Phillips living in Thurston County among the white population with three-year-old Maggie and one-year-old Tom. At some point, she moved to the Lummi Reservation where she spent the rest of her life. Perhaps she had had enough of white society. She died in 1920 and her family buried her in the reservation cemetery in an unmarked grave.

Her son Mason Fitzhugh and his family are buried on Orcas Island in the traditional Lummi burial ground. Her descendants still live among the Lummi, Samish, Swinomish, and S'Klallam.

The community of Langdon on Orcas Island, near the lime kiln where George Phillips worked, where Xwelas killed her violent husband, and where her babies died on that terrible day, is now abandoned.

6

Assassination on Lake Washington (1886)

On a February morning in 1886, Mrs. Clarissa Colman watched her husband row across Lake Washington, heading southwest from their farm on the eastern shore. James Colman had one passenger in his skiff, a lad in his late teens named Wilbur Patten. Clarissa continued to watch from her window as the men crossed the frigid winter waters until they disappeared around the southern tip of Mercer Island.

That night, James did not return as expected from his trip to Seattle. Clarissa was not concerned. Rowing to the Jackson Street wharf was a rigorous business, and James was due to testify in court that day. A delay in his return was not expected but was not surprising either.

Fifty-year-old James was well-known and highly regarded among settlers in the area. Ten years earlier, the Colman family had relocated to Washington Territory from Savannah, Georgia, where James had worked in the customs service, a laudable appointment by President Grant. He and Clarissa and their four children settled on 160 acres on the eastern shore of the lake in today's Kennydale area. He planted 20 acres, keeping the rest as woodland. Twice, he was elected to the Board of County Commissioners and had also served recently on a grand jury.

Wilbur Patten, the young man riding in the skiff, was a student who boarded in Seattle with his sister, Laura. He had been traveling around Lake Washington with a friend and spent Sunday night with the Colman family. James Colman had offered him a ride back to Seattle.

It was Laura Patten who first sounded the alarm when her brother did not return. She contacted a local man, John Mathiesen, who lived on Lake Washington, asking if he had seen Wilbur. Mathiesen grew alarmed because he had gone past the Colman home in his boat earlier and Mrs. Colman had flagged him down, asking the same question about her husband, last seen with Wilbur. Mathiesen headed back to the Colman home, where he and Clarissa concluded that something was wrong.

Mathiesen formed a search party. They rowed up and down the shores of Lake Washington and Mercer Island, scanning the beaches and dense brush for any sign of the missing men.

On Friday, February 12, four days after James Colman and Wilbur Patten set off for Seattle, searchers discovered the skiff. The scene looked bad. The skiff was beached on the west side of Mercer Island, directly opposite the Mathiesen home in Seattle. Blood smeared the wooden seats. They found Colman's bloody coat and his dentures. The two oars were also blood-stained. They saw no sign of James or young Wilbur. In a move that would be sure to aggravate modern investigators, the men towed the skiff to the Jackson Street wharf. Mathiesen stayed with the skiff while others searched for the sheriff.

At that time, the situation in Seattle was extremely tense. The city was reeling from a four-day riot on the part of white laborers agitating to expel Chinese workers. Roving gangs affiliated with the Knights of Labor had forcibly driven 200 Chinese residents from the city, and five people had been seriously injured. The riots had finally calmed down on Sunday, the day before Colman headed to Seattle.

Despite the circumstances, Sheriff John McGraw took action when the search party told him about the boat and the missing men. He contacted Wilbur's school, where the principal confirmed that Wilbur was indeed missing and that they had been extremely worried about him. The principal insisted that Wilbur was a reliable young man, not the type to vanish.

McGraw immediately fixed on a suspect, George Miller, and two of his sons. Miller was a local farmer with a wife and seven children. His two eldest sons were William, eighteen, and John, sixteen, who seemed to split their time between the family home and the coal mines of Newcastle. George Miller had a bad reputation around the lake region and was dubbed by the press as "Pirate Miller."

According to Clarissa Colman, there had long been animosity between the Millers and Colmans. The trouble started soon after the Colmans arrived in Washington Territory. Clarissa had accused George Miller of stealing, and he had returned the insult by accusing her of the same. The issue had never been resolved and the two families had been at odds ever since.

On that fateful Monday morning when James and Wilbur disappeared, both James Colman and George Miller were scheduled to appear in court in Seattle. One of the Miller boys, possibly John, had also been subpoenaed to appear, reportedly to face charges of trying to claim a tract of timberland before he reached legal age. Locals accused George of using his son's name to get hold of extra land. Colman went to Seattle to testify against Miller. Miller showed up without his son, and Colman never appeared.

Armed with this information, Sheriff McGraw organized a posse and they set out in a lake steamer called *The Bee* for the Miller farm, located between Beaux Arts and Enatai on the eastern shore of Lake Washington. That Friday night, the posse surrounded the Miller home, ready for trouble. But the Millers let the sheriff in without resistance.

Confronted about the disappearance of the two men, George Miller acted nervous and pretended that he didn't know who Colman was. He complained about the case and told the sheriff that he and his boys were just trying to get along and make a living but that "bad neighbors" were trying to hurt them. The oldest boy, William, was in the home and he told the sheriff that his brother John was working at the Newcastle Coal Mine.

Sheriff McGraw arrested both George and William Miller and hauled them to jail in Seattle. McGraw later testified that the Miller family came for a visit:

[Miller] raised both hands and warn[ed] them from him, said vehemently, rapidly and in a very excited manner: "Don't you open your mouths here! Don't you say a word here! If anyone comes around the place drive them away. Don't talk to them. Don't say a word to anybody except my attorneys. Don't send me anything. I have everything that I want here."[1]

For the time being, anyway, George Miller's consternation was unnecessary. The magistrate soon released him and William for lack of evidence. After that, the case came to a standstill. Locals began dragging the lake, looking for the bodies of James and Wilbur.

A local woman, Mrs. Frank Dusharm, had told her husband that she had a vivid dream the night the men disappeared. She said the dream showed her where the bodies would be found. She did not know where it was, but she described the spot she had seen in her dream.

Perhaps Mrs. Dusharm's dream led the men to a certain place as some claimed, or perhaps it is just a Lake Washington legend, but on March 5, a group of determined men found some clues. First, they spotted Wilbur Patten's coat, and then, a few days later, they found his hat.

They focused their search on that area, which was 3 miles south of where they found the skiff. They rigged up a dragging apparatus using a 19-foot pole with a hook on the end. Someone put together a "sort of tube with which a person can see in deep water."[2] They rowed along the shore, dragging the pole, hoping it would catch on something. Finally, it did.

[W]e all of a sudden came up on Patten's body, in 15 feet of water, lying face up. With my long pole and hook we hauled his body to the surface and placed it in the boat. We resumed our search, and 10 feet further on lay the body of James Manning Colman, in about the same depth of water. As we drew his body to the surface we saw a great hole in his left temple … These bodies were found within a hundred yards of the southwest point of the island, and not more than 160 yards from where the men passed out of Mrs. Colman's view on that fatal February morning.[3]

The men sent word to Mrs. Colman, then rowed the bodies to Seattle.

The *post-mortem* confirmed they had finally found James Colman and Wilbur Patten, nearly a month after their disappearance. Each had been shot twice with a .40-60 Winchester, and it appeared that the second shots occurred sometime after the first. Colman had two rifle ball wounds in his head, one through the left temple, and another in the top of the head, ranging downward. Patten was shot through the leg and through the torso. The latter bullet had severed his spine.

Wilbur's silver watch had stopped at 7:05. He had a knife and a half dollar. In Colman's vest pockets were a pocketbook, two $5 gold pieces, and a $5 bill. His watch was missing.

Sheriff McGraw headed once again to the Miller farm and arrested the father. During the ride back in the steamer, McGraw decided to test Miller's reaction. He directed the pilot to run the steamer close by the spot where they found the bodies. As they passed by, Miller looked away. McGraw asked the pilot to turn back and head into the beach. McGraw later testified:

> Just as the keel was touching the shore the prisoner jumped from his seat, and raised his elbow against the pilot house, and rested his head on his hand in about this manner, [indicating,] and fastened his eyes on the deck of the boat. He was trembling violently, his whole frame showing intense mental excitement.[4]

McGraw also said that the first time he arrested Miller, he had noticed a .40-60 Winchester in the farmhouse. The second time, he could not find the Winchester.

In November 1886, George Miller went on trial in Port Townsend for the murders of James Colman and Wilbur Patten. Residents testified about seeing Miller on the day before the murder, a Sunday, rowing around the island, ostensibly "casing" the area in preparation for the assassination. This was contradicted by the Knight family, Miller's neighbor in the Mercer slough area, who had fed him a midday meal that Sunday.

Locals said they heard gunshots at 7 a.m. on Monday morning, the day the men disappeared. Two witnesses said they were at the Miller farmhouse that morning and insisted that Miller did not leave the house until after 8 a.m.

Defense attorneys argued that, even if the 7 a.m. gunshots were unrelated to the murders, Miller did not have time to leave his farm at 8 a.m., row down to the southern tip of Mercer Island, shoot the two men, and then make it to the hearing in Seattle by 10 a.m.

Others testified about seeing a mysterious figure in a black boat near the scene of the murder, and that Miller was known to be the only person on Lake Washington to own a black boat. One nine-year-old girl testified that she saw a female in a black boat near the murder scene, which cast some suspicion on Miller's daughter, Lizzie.

Defense and prosecution attorneys argued at length about how long it took to row from one place to another. They had a long discussion about how much perspiration George Miller generated on any given occasion and how much perspiration would indicate a guilty anxiety. The defense suggested that the anxious behavior that witnesses reported could be attributed to his general ignorance and illiteracy. At the end of the trial, the jury could not agree on a verdict.

The following spring, in April 1887, a Seattle court held a second trial. This jury also failed to agree on a verdict. However, in June of the same year, at Miller's third trial, a jury of Kitsap County citizens found Miller guilty of the double murder. The judge sentenced him to hang on September 23.

Miller's shifting fortunes were still not settled. In September, the governor granted Miller a stay of execution. In February 1888, the Supreme Court of the Territory of Washington overturned the guilty verdict. The gist of their argument was that the case against Miller was purely circumstantial and that it was not strong enough for a conviction.

Yet another trial, Miller's fourth, was held in April 1888, but the judge dismissed the case for lack of evidence. George Miller returned to his farm, ostensibly a free man. He and his family were drained, emotionally and financially. Some of their neighbors did not agree with the court's latest ruling, and they hounded the family. Someone burned down Lizzie's house, perhaps those who suspected she had been the shooter. Lizzie was known to be a good shot with a rifle.

During the years after the murder, the elder son, William Miller, was in and out of the insane asylum at Steilacoom. In October 1891, William attacked the farmhouse of the Knight family—the folks who had fed his father a meal, providing him with an alibi during the time when he was supposedly "casing" the island. William shot into the Knight home through a window and hacked down the front door with an ax. His motive was never explained. He also set fire to another neighbor's farmhouse and shot two of that family's cows. William told an official that his father was guilty of the murders and that the murder weapon, the missing Winchester, was at the bottom of Lake Washington.

Sometime during this same period, another Miller child, their daughter Josephine, committed suicide. Five years after being cleared of the murders, in 1893, George Miller died of a stroke.

The Colman family fared better. Clarissa Colman, who kept a diary during those years, supported her family by selling beef, pork, hay, plus fruits and vegetables and butter to the company store at the nearby Newcastle coal mines. She also invested in real estate in Seattle.

Clarissa died in 1919 at age seventy-seven. Her son, George, and his wife continued farming on the Colman homestead. The family eventually donated Clarissa's diaries to the Eastside Heritage Center in Bellevue, where they serve as an important historical record of the area.

For years, many on Mercer Island referred to the island's southern tip as Murder Point. The place where searchers found the skiff became Deadman's Bay. The murder weapon was never found, although some years later, a Winchester .40-60 was found hidden in a barn being razed in Wilburton.

7

A Vaudevillian Tale (1901)

For an entire day, former Chief of Police William Meredith prowled the streets of Seattle. Wrapped in butcher paper and tucked under his arm was a double-barreled, sawed-off shotgun loaded with buckshot. He carried three revolvers and a dirk stashed in his pockets. Late that Tuesday afternoon, he ran into a friend and asked him if he had seen John Considine, a well-known "box theater" operator in town. The friend noticed the package under Meredith's arm and urged him not to do anything rash. Meredith told him, vaguely, that he would "take care of the consequences," and went on his way.

Meredith had only been the former chief for a few days, since the mayor of Seattle, Thomas J. Humes, had demanded his resignation on Saturday night, June 22, 1901. As far as Meredith was concerned, John Considine had been trying to destroy him for a long time, and he had finally succeeded. Meredith wanted revenge.

Around 5:30 p.m., he finally spotted Considine standing in front of Guy's drugstore at the corner of Yesler and Second Avenue. What happened next would create a massive uproar in the city of Seattle and shatter many lives.

William Luff Meredith came from an upper-class home in Washington, D.C. His father was Captain William Meredith, chief of the Bureau of Engraving and Printing under President Harrison. The younger William, born in 1868, was educated in Chicago and came west to Seattle at age twenty, working in the lucrative real estate business.

In 1891, he married Nellie Jennings in Vancouver, B.C., and the couple had two children, Russell and Dorothy. Meredith left the real estate business and became a customs inspector at the port of Seattle. He also befriended and worked for the vaudeville promoter John Considine and accompanied him to Spokane for a few years. After that, he returned to police work in Seattle and became a detective. By most accounts, he was respected and well-liked.

As a policeman, Meredith enjoyed an excellent reputation for his courage and composure under pressure. In 1897, he distinguished himself in the highly publicized case of a murderer and desperado named Charles Phillips. An officer named James Wells had arrested Phillips for murder and was escorting him into the jailhouse. Apparently still armed, Phillips pulled his gun, shot Wells, and took off running. Gravely injured, Wells went after him and fired one shot at him. Phillips turned and shot Wells again, which killed him.

Meredith and another detective, Lee Barbee, were inside the police station when they heard the shots. They ran out and saw Wells fall. They continued pursuing Phillips, who turned again and continued firing. A third detective joined the pursuit, which erupted into a gun battle on Washington Avenue near Fourth, during which Phillips escaped.

Meredith and Barbee continued searching for the shooter. A small boy told them he had heard a strange noise under an empty building. The detectives found a lantern and crept into the crawl space. Barbee spotted a figure among the shadows and ordered him to come out. As Phillips raised his arm to shoot, both detectives fired. One shot blasted the killer's weapon from his hand and the detectives quickly subdued him.

Back at the station, they discovered that Barbee's shot had hit Phillips in the leg and Meredith's .44 caliber bullet had pierced the man's wrist and knocked his weapon away. Phillips's hand had to be amputated. He was later sentenced to twelve years for manslaughter and was released in 1906.

Meredith, meanwhile, continued his impressive career in the police department. After one temporary demotion, which Meredith blamed on Considine's efforts to sabotage him, Mayor Thomas Humes appointed him chief of police in 1900.

John Considine had grown up in Chicago, the son of an Irish-Catholic saloon keeper. His history reportedly included a stint as a Chicago policeman, during which he participated in the police shooting of striking workers that led to the infamous Haymarket Riot of 1886. He left Chicago soon after, briefly attending college in Kansas. After a couple of school terms, he took work as an actor with a traveling stock company.

He landed in Seattle in 1889. There, he began his lifelong career as an entertainment entrepreneur. Although he personally enjoyed a reputation as a sober man and a "square gambler" who could be trusted in business affairs, his operations over the years wobbled back and forth between legitimate and illegitimate. His enterprises included "box houses," gambling dens, and eventually a chain of vaudeville theaters. A box house was basically a bordello disguised as a theater, featuring curtained "boxes" where male patrons could get serviced by female "entertainers" while cheap theatricals might or might not be unfolding on stage.

His personal life was tumultuous. Back in Chicago, in 1884, he had married at twenty-one years old to Julia Nussbaumer. They had a daughter, Agnes, born in 1888. By 1890, he and Julia had divorced, and he had remarried to Elizabeth Donnellan, to whom his daughter, Francine, was born in 1890.

The divorce from Julia was deeply contentious and she would not allow him to see Agnes. In 1892, police arrested John Considine for abducting four-year-old Agnes from Julia's home in Seattle. That day, he had watched Julia's house, waiting for her to go out. When she left, he knocked on the door and spun a story to Julia's friend, Mrs. Dudley, who was watching Agnes. He told her he had come to inform Julia that he was ready to pay the money he owed her and resolve their differences. Mrs. Dudley told him that Julia was out, so he asked to see Agnes.

Agnes was reportedly not interested in seeing her father, but Mrs. Dudley carried her downstairs to Considine as he waited in the parlor. He then told Mrs. Dudley to fetch Agnes's coat and boots so he could take her on an outing to get some candy. Mrs. Dudley said "no."

Considine grew angry, retorting that Agnes was his. He picked up the child and headed for the door. Mrs. Dudley grabbed Agnes around the waist, and Considine dragged the pair—woman and child—to the front door. He jerked the door open so violently that Mrs. Dudley and Agnes flew across the porch. Agnes landed with a thud, smacking her forehead.

Two nearby women screamed for help and neighbors quickly gathered around the porch. After some discussion, Mrs. Dudley decided to calm the situation. She and Considine each took one of Agnes's hands, and together, they walked the child to a candy store one block away, where Considine bought his daughter gum and candy and gave her a $5 gold piece. He then walked away.

Police later arrested him for attempted kidnapping and the case went to trial. However, the judge immediately dismissed the charge:

> The defense introduced no testimony, but moved for a dismissal, which the justice granted, saying that it appeared to him that Considine had no intention to kidnap the child and that his conduct was entirely consistent with innocence.[1]

The year 1893 was another bad one for Considine. A local newspaper editor criticized his business and supposedly tried to extort money from him. Considine went after the man, kicked him, and punched him in the jaw. It is unknown whether he faced charges for the attack.

Later that year, authorities raided a crap game he operated in the basement of his establishment, the People's theater. Two men named Wilson and Cameron were slated to testify against him. He bribed Cameron to get out of town and forget about testifying. Cameron agreed to the deal, and he also agreed to lure Wilson to a meeting with Considine. Wilson, however, was not having it and tried to walk out of the meeting. According to Wilson, Considine followed him and punched him in the face:

> [Then, he] either kicked or hit me on the other side, cutting my ear and my cheek. I offered no resistance but kept on going downstairs. Considine followed me and hit me another lick, near the foot of the stairs. After I got out on the sidewalk they threw my hat out after me and told me to screw.[2]

Meanwhile, back in Chicago, John's older brother, Thomas Considine, was operating saloons and gaming houses in the levee district, a rough part of town. Thomas had gotten an early start in the business, already working as a bartender (presumably in his father's saloon) at age fourteen. The Considines had garnered considerable bad press in Chicago and at some point, Tom quit the saloon business and became a bookie at a racecourse at Roby, Indiana. However, his reputation there was also marred by rumors of fixed races. Police raided the track and arrested betting officials. Eventually, the track closed under the weight of the scandals, and then it burned down. Tom Considine headed west to join his brother in Seattle.

During much of the 1890s, John Considine and William Meredith were political allies. Meredith worked for Considine at one point, though it is not clear what his job was, and by some accounts, the two were partners in a gambling business.

Not surprisingly, their relationship soured due to Meredith's flourishing career in the Seattle Police Department. He advanced to detective and began enforcing laws that Considine did not care for. In no time, Meredith stepped on Considine's toes. Considine was a consummate player and he was accustomed to a great deal of cooperation from city government and law enforcement.

The Klondike Gold Rush of the late 1890s created a rowdy atmosphere in Seattle and business was booming for the bordellos, gambling house and saloons. The Thomas Humes administration (1897–1904) was one of amiable tolerance for Seattle's underbelly. The general approach was to collect monthly "fines" from those businesses who broke laws against gambling, prostitution, child labor, and other seamy activities.

Considine accused Meredith of selective enforcement, of singling him out by arresting only friends and colleagues of Considine's. He also claimed that Meredith had been collecting fines and pocketing them himself.

In 1899, Meredith arrested a friend of Considine's for being a pickpocket. Angered, Considine prevailed upon his good buddy, Chief of Police C. S. Reed, to reduce Meredith's rank from detective to front desk clerk. This humiliation lasted several months. At the turn of the century, Meredith regained his position as detective, and when Reed left office in 1900, Mayor Humes appointed Meredith chief of police.

The newly appointed chief geared up for renewed battle against Considine. The war went on for another year and a half. It finally landed in the courts in May 1901, when Meredith arrested a black newspaper editor, Horace R. Cayton, publisher of *The Weekly Republican*.

Cayton was the son of a slave and a white woman, born on a Mississippi plantation in 1859 to the plantation owner's daughter. After emancipation, he attended college and headed west, where he worked for a couple of newspapers before starting his own in partnership with his wife, Susie Revels. Cayton was a vocal critic of the anything-goes atmosphere of the Klondike Gold Rush, the vice houses, and the "collect a monthly fine" policies of Mayor Humes.

Meredith had previously tried to recruit Cayton to his side in the battle against Considine, assuring him that Considine and Reed were at the heart of the city's corruption. However, Cayton apparently grew disenchanted with this narrative and published a column to that effect: "It is up to Chief Meredith to rid the city of these grafting policemen, but perhaps if that were done we should be rid of Chief Meredith himself."[3]

Meredith immediately arrested Cayton, charging him with criminal libel. The trial, which began right away, quickly mutated into the latest setting for another battle between Considine and Meredith, consisting of back and forth accusations between the two men and Cayton apparently caught between the two.

Called to testify first off, Considine looked like a no-show until he arrived at the last minute, after which he gabbled on at great length, apparently basking in the spotlight. He gave remarkably candid testimony about his various money-making schemes and the amount in bribes he paid to city officials. He claimed that the People's theater had served as a hub for secret police pay-offs from "thieves and men of the under-world." He described how these other scurrilous characters left money for Meredith or used Considine's premises to pay Meredith directly.

Under questioning, he admitted that, some years earlier, he had been forced to leave Seattle for a time and start over in Spokane after a prize fighter had been killed at his place. He also admitted that Spokane city officials had run him out of town in 1897 and that he had returned to Seattle to try again.

He boasted about his chumminess with prior police chiefs, testifying that former Chief of Police Bolton Rogers had given him $300 for an interest in a gambling house. He claimed he had paid former Chief of Police Reed $1,000 a week.

He described his falling out with Meredith over a man named Harper, who had been "a great money-getter for Meredith." However, Meredith had arrested him.

Yes, and right there me and Meredith had a falling out. Harper was a friend of mine, and Meredith, who had been sharing in his spoils, had him arrested for stealing $36 in a big mit joint [a card room that cheats players or allows players to cheat each other]. Meredith got his regular 10 per cent., $3.60, out of this money, and then had him arrested. I believe in honor among thieves and I wouldn't stand for that sort of thing.[4]

He had not spoken to Meredith since that time and told a *Seattle Star* reporter: "I am going to do Meredith, and don't care who it hurts or what happens."[5]

He confessed that he had prevailed upon former Chief of Police Reed to remove Meredith from his position as detective and demote him to clerk at police headquarters. However, he said, others had pressed him to let up, and so he did, and thus Meredith was allowed back into the detective department.

Yet, he complained, Meredith permitted thieves and crooks to "run the town" instead of supporting Considine in the favored position he had previously enjoyed (running the town himself). He insisted that he had gone to Meredith and tried to convince him to "be square" and shut down the others. He proclaimed to the court that he had been in a desperate fight for self-preservation.

When Meredith took the stand, he denied Considine's claims and stated emphatically that he did not personally collect fines from illegal operators. "Those people are prosecuted monthly and fined in court," he said. He insisted that the fines were paid to the city, not to individual police officers or city officials.

After Meredith testified, the president of a newly minted group, the Law and Order League, took the stand. E. L. Blaine and his supporters, mostly clergy and prohibitionists, were determined to rid Seattle of its seamier elements. He said he had drawn up a list of unacceptable businesses in town and given it to Meredith, but that Meredith had not shut any of them down. However, he admitted that he had no knowledge that Meredith had personally profited or collected any fines himself.

Finally, Cayton himself came to the stand. He described the conversations he had shared with Meredith back when Reed was chief of police. Meredith had told him that Considine had been "appointed chief of the gamblers and he and Chief Reed arranged what places should run and what should not."[6]

"Meredith told me that whenever I saw a gambler personally arrested and brought to court, it would mean that he was not paying blackmail to the police," said Cayton.[7] Since then, Cayton had been investigating the payoffs. He had grown disenchanted with Meredith when the latter allowed the businesses to continue operating as long as they paid the fines.

After Cayton finished testifying, an unexpected witness took the stand. Mrs. Ross was a medium and fortune teller who had paid fines to the city.

She testified that a Detective Crane had come to her business and she gave him a reading. He then told her that Meredith wanted to see her. She went to see him, "and he told me I would have to get out of town or quit the business. That I would have to put up $50. I said I would think it over."

> On cross examination it was brought out that Meredith had told her that she was under arrest, and that unless she promised to give up her business, she would be required to give $50 for her appearance in court. That she had promised to abandon her business, and had been allowed to go with a warning.[8]

Meredith took the stand again, saying that Mrs. Ross had been arrested with many other fortune tellers and that he had taken the same course with all of them. The chief said:

> In every case where the women promised to give up the business ... I made no complaint against them. In this instance I told Mrs. Ross she must promise to give up the business, and that if she would not make that promise, she would have to deposit $50 cash bail for her appearance in court. She said she would stop, and I told her to go home.[9]

On May 25, the case went to the jury, but they were unable to reach a verdict. Presiding Judge George Meade Emory discharged the jury and announced that the case would be retried once they cleared a number of murder cases from the docket. However, the case would never come to court again.

Within a few days of the Cayton trial, the city council formed a new committee called the "Lexow committee" to investigate police corruption, specifically focusing on Meredith. Although the committee tried to operate in secret, much of its doings were leaked to the press.

Considine had promised to bring a series of witnesses that would shock the committee but when it was time for him to come and testify, they couldn't find him. Finally, on June 5, Considine arrived and testified for three hours. He reiterated his previous claims and gave several more instances where he witnessed Meredith taking money. He said a man named Chester Edwards had paid Meredith $30 and that Ben Pincus had also paid money to Meredith. He produced a letter that Meredith had written in 1895 saying that Considine was a man of his word.

On June 19, Meredith was called to testify, and once again, he denied all charges. He had an affidavit from Chester Edwards wherein he admitted that Considine had instructed him to try to bribe Meredith, but that Meredith had thrown him out of his office. Another man was brought in to see the committee and testified that Considine had manufactured the Pincus charge.

Meredith told the committee that John Considine had "ruined" a female contortionist who worked at the People's theater and that she had undergone a "criminal operation" (an illegal abortion). Considine was ready for this and had on hand affidavits from both the girl and the doctor denying the charge and that the contortionist had been in the hospital because of "muscular over-exertion."

On Friday night, June 21, the Lexow committee gave its report to Mayor Humes. Despite the testimony from Meredith and others contradicting what Considine had told them, they had apparently chosen, for unknown reasons, to believe Considine instead of Meredith. They stated simply that "Mr. Meredith's character will not be assailed, nor will the report indicate the finding of the committee further than to file a justifiable recommendation for his removal."[10]

On Saturday, Mayor Humes asked Meredith to resign, and Meredith did so reluctantly. He said:

> I asked for a fair, open investigation, and did not get it. I now ask anyone who can come forward and say anything derogatory to my character, to do so. If it has been alleged that I have been a bribe-taker, why don't these accusers come out open and above board, and then, if they are to believed, let someone prosecute me criminally in the courts.[11]

Mayor Humes refused to comment. The following Tuesday, William L. Meredith wrapped his shotgun in paper, stuffed the other weapons in his pockets, and set out to find John Considine.

At around 5:30 p.m. he spotted Considine outside Guy's drugstore at the corner of Second Avenue and Yesler Way. Considine was talking to a police officer, A. H. Metford, another enemy of Meredith's. Meredith crept up behind Metford, slid the wrapped shotgun onto the latter's shoulder, and fired at Considine's face. The butcher paper interfered with the shot and it knocked Considine's hat off but missed him.

Considine bolted into the crowded drugstore. Meredith followed, firing his second barrel. The shot again went mostly wild, this time spattering buckshot into the walls and ceiling and into the arm of a bystander, G. W. Houston. A single piece of buckshot smashed into John Considine's head at the base of his skull.

Meredith tossed the shotgun away and pulled a revolver from his pocket. Considine had dashed to the rear of the store where he found no escape. He turned to fight. His brother, Tom, appeared and the two men grappled with Meredith, trying to wrestle the revolver away from him. Meredith held the revolver high over his head but Tom, much larger than Meredith, got hold of it. He smashed the handgun into Meredith's head over and over. A detective named Lane tried to stop him, but Tom shoved him away and threatened to shoot him. John screamed, "Give it to him, Tom. Give it to him, Tom."[12]

Others finally pulled the three men apart. Reeling from his head wounds, Meredith staggered across the store and leaned against a showcase, his head drooping, his arms hanging limp. Officer Tommy Bevan had hold of him around the waist, propping him up, but Meredith began to sink. John Considine shoved the muzzle of his .38 caliber revolver against Meredith's limp body and fired repeatedly into his head and chest. Meredith's coat caught fire from the muzzle and Bevan snuffed it out with his hands. Meredith fell dead.

Officers had arrived quickly from the police station upstairs from Guy's Drugstore, but not fast enough to stop the shooting. The drugstore was smashed up. Someone took G. W. Houston to the hospital to be treated for the gunshot to his arm. Butterworth's mortuary arrived with the dead wagon and took Meredith's body to the morgue. Outside, the street was packed with people talking excitedly. Police arrested John and Tom Considine.

Seattle was in an uproar. Mayor Humes had left town after accepting Meredith's resignation but the newly appointed chief of police, John Sullivan, made a statement:

> Meredith's poor wife and children. His tragic death will mean everything to them. They have all my sympathy. The dead man was full of good traits and I held a high estimate of him. News of his death has brought me most intense pain and a sense of personal loss.[13]

A member of the committee that had recommended ousting Meredith, Councilman James, refused to discuss the shooting. "I always want to be away from trouble," he said. "I haven't a word to say more."[14]

Mrs. Nellie Meredith was at home at 923 26th Avenue South when someone phoned her with the news of her husband's death. Neighbors then filled the house, telling reporters that she was prostrate with grief. Their children, Dorothy, six, and Russell, nine, were also in the house.

Former city detective, C. W. Wappenstein, whom Considine had also accused of taking bribes, hastened to the Meredith residence. He made a statement to reporters:

> Of course I expected trouble between Considine and Meredith as soon as they met. Personally I cannot speak too highly of the ex-chief. His recent trouble may have prejudiced a few minds against him but to his friends no taint ever touched his character.[15]

Elizabeth Considine went to see her husband in jail where he was being treated for the injury to his scalp. Tom was uninjured.

An autopsy revealed that Meredith had suffered seven head wounds and his skull was fractured in two places. John Considine had shot him three times. A rumor circulated that the bystander, Houston, would likely lose his arm. That night, there was talk in Seattle of lynching the Considines. Meanwhile, Chief Sullivan fired Officer Metford for disappearing when the trouble started. It came out that Meredith had suspended Metford the previous March for pocketing fines he collected.

That same week, crowds gathered in front of the mortuary as the coroner's jury met. Numerous witnesses testified and a discrepancy arose about the number of shots fired. During the trial, this would become an important issue.

The jury quickly charged John and Tom Considine with murder, referring to them as "the gamblers." Another paper referred to John Considine as a "variety dive keeper." The *Seattle Star* reported that had the jury not issued the indictments, "a storm of indignation would have burst over the jurors' heads."[16]

By mid-July, John was released on $20,000 bail and Tom on $2,500. What followed was months of delays, during which the charges against Tom Considine were dismissed. Finally, John's trial began on November 2, 1901.

The court had trouble seating a jury that satisfied both sides. Potential jurors had to describe their feelings about gambling, liquor, "box houses," and the related activities that the Considines were famous for.

During its opening statement, the prosecution outlined its dual prongs of attack. First, Meredith was unarmed and helpless from the head blows when he was shot three times, so John Considine did not shoot him in self-defense. They also claimed that many witnesses had heard six shots, not the five claimed by the defense. They said that Meredith's two shotgun blasts were actually the second and third shots and the last three were from John Considine's revolver. The first shot, they said, had been delivered by a mysterious figure outside who then ran away down an alley. This shot, they said, was intended for Meredith, not Considine, which meant that Meredith's gunshots were a matter of self-defense.

The defense countered that many witnesses also said they heard only five shots: the first two from Meredith's shotgun and the last three from John Considine's revolver. They also contended that only thirty seconds elapsed between Tom hitting Meredith on the head and John shooting him, which meant there was not enough time for John to comprehend in the heat of the moment that Meredith had been overcome. Furthermore, they said that John believed that Meredith, instead of drooping his head, was looking down to draw another handgun.

The trial lasted sixteen days. Much of the testimony came from witnesses, very few of whom could agree how the gun battle had played out, how many shots were fired, or who did what. Both sides called witnesses who testified that each man had made threats against the other before the shooting. The ongoing war between the two men was reviewed exhaustively, including arguments about who was corrupt and who was not. There were, however, two points of general agreement: Meredith armed himself and went looking for Considine, and the Considine brothers kept "killing" Meredith when he was likely already dead.

On November 21, the case finally went to the jury. After three hours of deliberation, they informed the judge they had a verdict, and the courtroom filled again. Mrs. Meredith and her children had left the courtroom but the Considine family was still there to hear the jury's verdict: John Considine was not guilty.

Once the trial ended, it took some time for things to settle back down in the city. Rumors circulated that the Considines would no longer be allowed to operate, but after a short break, John reopened, and business at the People's theater went on as usual. He eventually opened a chain of vaudeville theaters and later moved to Los Angeles and entered the budding film industry. In later years, his sons followed him into the entertainment business. John Considine, Jr. became a Hollywood film producer, and the latter's sons, John and Tim Considine, both became Hollywood actors for television and screen.

The fate of Nellie Meredith and her children was marred by further tragedy. Nellie received a death benefit from her husband's policy with the Woodmen of the World, but about a year after William's death, on August 4, 1902, she died in San Francisco of pancreatitis. She left her young, now orphaned children in the care of William Meredith, Sr., of Washington D.C.

8

Honor Assassins
(1906)

Twenty-three-year-old George Mitchell was on the hunt. His quarry was a religious firebrand with a small but ardent cult following. Edmund Creffield had just finished serving a year at Oregon State Prison, found guilty of adultery with George's married sister, Donna. Edmund had convinced Donna that sexual intercourse with him was her religious duty. George's younger sister, eighteen-year-old Esther Mitchell, was also devoted to Creffield, despite the family's ongoing efforts to keep her away from him.

Soon after Edmund's release, Donna had run off with him again, abandoning her husband and several young children for the second time. George Mitchell had promised his little nieces and nephews that he would bring their mother back.

George was not the only man hunting for Edmund Creffield. A group of angry vigilantes had mobilized in Corvallis, Oregon, mostly consisting of family members who had lost someone to the Creffield cult. Edmund had gone into hiding, but George had a plan. He began following Edmund's wife, Maud Hurt Creffield. When she boarded a train from Portland to Seattle, he followed her there the next day.

After five days of searching, on the morning of May 7, he spotted both Maud and Edmund walking up a Seattle street. He ducked into a doorway and waited. As the couple strolled by, George leaped out, screamed "Creffield!" and shot the man in the head. Edmund died instantly with a .22 caliber bullet lodged in his brain.

George did not run but waited for authorities to arrive while Maud Creffield wailed over the body of her dead husband. Later, from the police station, he cabled Maud's father, his close friend O. V. Hurt back in Corvallis, Oregon and told him, "I got my man. Am now in jail." There were very few in Corvallis who did not rejoice at the news.

It is not clear how much of the legend about the Creffield cult was true and how much was hysterical exaggeration. The cult took root in Corvallis, Oregon in 1903, though it never boasted more than about twenty-five followers, mostly women. The group's noisy worship habits originated in the Holy Rollerism of the Salvation Army, with boisterous gatherings where followers rolled on the floor in religious ecstasy. Edmund Creffield himself was a former captain in the Salvation Army and it was they who sent him initially to Corvallis.

He eventually left the Salvation Army in favor of his own cult, having decided that he had special dispensation from God. Rumors soon spread through town that the Creffieldites worshipped the devil, ran around naked, engaged in sex orgies, and sacrificed household pets.

One of Creffield's demands was that his followers turn their backs on their families and devote themselves entirely to him. His married female acolytes neglected their duties as wife and mother. It is not clear how many obliged Creffield's demand for a purity ritual that involved sexual intercourse.

Edmund was a scrawny, homely, little man, weighing about 135 pounds, who reportedly immigrated from Germany about fifteen years prior. Despite his physical limitations, he possessed enough charisma to garner extreme loyalty from some of his followers.

One of his most devout acolytes was Esther Mitchell, who was only fifteen years old when she first joined the cult. Both Esther and her sister Donna were perfectly willing to abandon everything for him. The Mitchell family had been raised mostly motherless—Esther was only six when her mother died. A strict, unaffectionate father had then raised the children on his own. It is likely that the two women enjoyed an unusual degree of attention from Edmund that they never got at home.

When Creffield first began gathering followers in 1903 Corvallis, the townspeople did not know how to respond. The orgies and pet sacrifices may have been exaggerations, but witnesses and newspapers documented other extreme behaviors in detail. Neighbors watched in stunned silence in late October when the cultists, saying they rejected earthly possessions, dragged the contents of O. V. Hurt's home out into the yard and burned the lot of it in a giant bonfire. The cultists then repeated this religious extravaganza at another Corvallis home. The people of Corvallis were perplexed, shocked, and finally enraged.

On January 4, 1904, a group of men got hold of Edmund Creffield and one of his male followers. They tarred and feathered the two men and marched them through town before sending them on their way outside the city limits. The *Corvallis Gazette* published an opinion piece extolling the virtues of honor killings, likely as a warning to Edmund Creffield. Edmund made himself scarce, but not before marrying his most devout follower, young Maud Hurt, whose father's earthly possessions had just gone up in flames.

Oddly, Maud did not go into hiding with her husband but returned to her father's house, where townsfolk kept an eye on her. Around this time, word got out about Edmund's sexual relationship with Donna (Mitchell) Starr. Donna's husband, Burt, filed a criminal complaint of adultery against Creffield, and authorities began searching for him.

Meanwhile, George Mitchell had long seen himself as Esther's guardian in the absence of their father back in Illinois. He had already sent young Esther to live at the Boys and Girls Aid Society Home in Portland, in essence committing her to an institution where she had no freedom of movement. Upset about the tar and feather episode, Esther ran away from the boys and girls home in February 1904. George caught up with her and this time sent her back to her father in Illinois.

Other townspeople used similar tactics to "deprogram" their Creffieldite family members. Irate family heads sent five women and one man to the insane asylum and three young women to the Boys and Girls Aid Society Home.

Meanwhile, Edmund secretly returned to Corvallis and inexplicably installed himself in a dirty cubbyhole beneath the Hurt home. The move proved to be a foolish one as his most ardent followers were off being "deprogrammed." Edmund, hiding underneath the house, was trapped and starving. One day, young Roy Hurt, a boy, was crawling around under the house and he heard a voice speak to him in broken English. The lad scampered away in terror and told his father about the scary voice under the house. O. V. Hurt notified the police.

Officers soon arrived and dragged Edmund out from under the house. He was so emaciated he could barely stand. They arrested him and charged him with adultery. While they escorted Edmund to jail and fed him, he muttered that he was a high priest and that he was Joshua from the Old Testament. He made other demented claims that both entertained and annoyed his jailers. They assumed he was trying to play crazy so he could "cheat the penitentiary."

Authorities treated Edmund to a speedy trial, during which he confessed to having sexual intercourse with Donna Starr. His defense was that he was merely following orders from God. The jury went out to deliberate and returned after fifteen minutes. They found him guilty and gave him the maximum sentence: two years in the State Penitentiary at Salem.

During Edmund's incarceration, the people of Corvallis gradually brought their "insane" family members back home. Edmund's wife, Maud Hurt Creffield, returned to her parents and divorced Edmund. Back in Illinois, Esther Mitchell also appeared to be cured of her mania and her father sent her back to Oregon, where she found a job. Edmund worked hard in prison on a road crew, which served him well, since each workday knocked two days off his sentence. After fifteen months, he was released.

In early 1906, the rumor circulated around Corvallis that Creffield was back. The townspeople kept a close eye on his former followers, even monitoring their mail. What they did not know was that seventeen-year-old Esther Mitchell had always remained true to her overlord and she was secretly helping Edmund gather his flock.

Edmund had turned his back on Corvallis and planned to establish a new compound on the coast, 90 miles west of the town. He lured Maud back into his arms and the pair remarried in April 1906. By that spring, he had reassembled about half of his former disciples. This included Donna Starr, who left home in the middle of the night to rejoin the man who had "spiritually cleansed" her.

One irate citizen, Lewis Hartley, caught his wife and daughter as they boarded a train to go to Creffield. He forced them off the train, but the women broke away from him and continued on foot to rejoin their master. Hartley bought a gun and headed out to the new camp on the coast. He spotted Creffield and fired, but the gun failed to go off. Hartley had to return home and procure another gun. By the time he returned to the coastal camp, Creffield had disappeared again.

Other Corvallis men joined the hunt. So many angry men with guns were looking for Creffield at this point that he had to abandon his plans for a Shangri-La and go back into permanent hiding. He fled to Seattle, which is where George Mitchell soon discovered and killed him.

After Edmund Creffield's death, the Seattle newspapers filled with sordid stories about Creffield and his followers. While the prosecution aimed to convict George of first-degree murder, a capital offense, a public narrative emerged that George had saved his family's reputation and protected his weak-minded sisters from a vile seducer. It was an honor killing. In the eyes of many, George Mitchell was a hero.

George worked hard to promote himself as such, talking to the press at every opportunity and recounting details about Creffield's "free love" cult. He said his actions were worth it, even if he were put to death. He blamed Creffield for making women so insane they had to be committed to the asylum. Finally, Seattle Chief of Police Charles Wappenstein told George he needed to shut up since his statements to the press could be used against him.

At the same time, the witness to the shooting, Maud Creffield, generally refused to talk to the press. However, when Edmund was buried, Maud and Esther swore that he would soon rise from the dead, a fact that local newspapers reported with great glee. As the trial drew near, Esther, who was slated to testify against her brother, was dismissed in the press as "unnatural." The Multnomah district attorney in Portland even wrote a letter to Seattle Prosecutor Kenneth Mackintosh and John F. Miller, his chief deputy, urging them not to try George Mitchell for murder.

The trial began on June 25. The defense delivered an opening statement that went on for four hours, while the prosecution's remarks lasted only ten minutes. The prosecution's case was simple, since George had shot Creffield in cold blood in broad daylight in front of witnesses, then had waited to be arrested. He did not deny that he had ambushed the Creffields and shot Edmund dead. George sat quietly, showing no emotion while the coroner described how the bullet cut through Edmund's spinal cord and lodged in his jaw, killing him instantly.

Maud took the stand and told the jury how George shot her husband as they walked down the street together. Reporters described her as crazy with religious fervor.

George's attorney, Silas Shipley, built his defense around Creffield's horrific behavior, and claimed that Creffield had driven George to temporary insanity. He talked about how Creffield called himself "Joshua," how he had seduced Donna Starr, and how groups of angry Corvallis men had been hunting him down at the time of the shooting. He said George's calm demeanor was a matter of his delusional state, and that George had told others that God had instructed him to kill Creffield.

The defense called both Esther Mitchell and Donna Starr, who gave testimony hostile to their brother. The defense attorney called them because he wanted the jury to see them as mentally weak and hopelessly under Creffield's influence.

O. V. Hurt, Maud's father, testified about what he had been through with his family and his home at the hands of Creffield. He came off as overwhelmed, in a state of emotional collapse. Weeping, he told the jury how Creffield had destroyed his family. He described the bonfires, the burning furniture, the sacrificed dogs and cats, the alienation of his daughter Maud as well as his wife, who was also a Creffield acolyte. He told how both women had ended up in the insane asylum because of Creffield. He described the day his frightened son had discovered a mangy-looking Creffield creeping around under his house.

Finally, Burt Starr, Donna's husband, testified. He narrated another horror story, describing his wife's adultery and incidents of her rolling around on the floor of their home wailing in fervent prayer. He told the court how she had deserted him and their three youngsters to follow Creffield to his new Shangri-La on the Oregon coast. He described how Uncle George had promised the little children that he would bring their mother back to them.

A flurry of other defense witnesses took the stand. Some averred that they also wanted to kill Creffield but George had beaten them to it. Others insisted that George had become increasingly unstable because of the Creffield stress and was out of his mind when he did the deed.

Late on a Tuesday afternoon, July 10, 1906, the case went to the jury. They deliberated for ninety minutes and their verdict brought cheers in the courtroom: George Mitchell was not guilty. George's supporters were overjoyed, but the judge hearing the case, Judge Frater, did not share the elation. He condemned the jury and the verdict, and said, quite accurately, that the killing had been a cold-blooded murder.

Two days later, George and two other brothers from the Mitchell family went to the station to catch a train back home to Corvallis. Among the well-wishers who came to see him off was George's sister, Esther. She told George she wanted to mend the rift in their family. After saying goodbye, George turned away to climb onto the train. Esther pulled out a pistol and shot her brother in the back of the head. The newly exonerated George Mitchell fell and died on the platform.

As George had done after he shot Edmund, Esther waited over the body for the police to arrest her. It soon emerged that she and Maud Creffield had purchased the gun together. Maud had gone looking for George to kill him but had been unable to find him, so Esther said she would shoot him. The city was stunned by the second shooting. Esther declared that she did not regret her action. Police arrested both Esther and Maud and put them in a cell together.

In September, Judge Frater appointed a commission of three men to decide whether or not the women were insane. The group concluded that they were both paranoid and suffered from "structural defects of the nervous system." The prosecution protested vehemently.

That November, Maud Creffield took a dose of strychnine and killed herself. Angry authorities demanded to know how she got hold of the strychnine, but Esther refused to say. Police suspected a visiting cousin, but they never resolved the case.

A few months later, in February 1907, authorities sent Esther to Western Washington Hospital for the Insane. After two years, she was released in March 1909, having been judged, once more, as "recovered."

She moved back to Oregon where she lived with the O. V. Hunt family for some years. In 1914, she married at age twenty-six and her life seemed to be taking a more moderate course. However, only a few months after her marriage, she also killed herself with a dose of strychnine.

9

A Dangerous Obsession
(1906)

Young Chester Thompson had numerous obsessions. He was fixated on food and refused to eat meat, which in 1906 was considered very strange indeed. For any given food item, he could tell you how long it took the stomach to digest it. He stored his personal food in a box that was off limits to the rest of the family. He worried about contamination, telling others that there could be poisons seeping through the shells into his private stash of eggs. In high school, he wrote extensively about "physical culture," which today would be called fitness, and he was known for walking around the streets of Seattle for hours, preferably at night, sometimes not returning home until dawn. Chester was an anti-vaxxer, insisting that he had bad teeth because his blood had been poisoned by vaccinations.

His father, the noted Seattle attorney, William H. Thompson, was skeptical of yet another of Chester's obsessions: photography. He ridiculed Chester's prescient view of photography as high art. He was particularly annoyed by Chester's habit of ordering thousands of dollars' worth of extravagant photographic equipment without permission. More than once, William Thompson cancelled orders after suppliers notified him about a huge bill that would soon arrive on his desk.

He was likely unimpressed when his son claimed to invent a special process for creating color photographs. Developed by the noted Lumière brothers in France, this process hit the market in 1907. Some said Chester was crazy; others called him "lovable." Many admired his notable intellect and dismissed his eccentricities as a case of bashfulness.

Unfortunately, when Chester was twenty-one, one of his obsessions devastated three prominent Seattle families, including his own: his infatuation with a pretty young lady named Charlotte Whittlesey.

Chester and Charlotte had known each other for several years. They met in 1902 during a five-week camping adventure at Lake Crescent on the Olympic

Peninsula. Another prominent family had invited Chester and his brother, Oscar, to join a large group of holidaymakers, and Charlotte and Chester became friends during that time. They danced, played croquet, and went on walks together. Afterward, Charlotte went away to the East Coast to continue her schooling. Chester stayed at home in Seattle, flunking out of his own studies at a local university and cranking out hundreds of poems in honor of the lovely Charlotte.

This was a period of great difficulty for the Thompson family. Chester's mother, Ida Thompson (*née* Lee), suffered a series of strokes and was paralyzed. She was slowly dying, largely unaware of what was going on around her. Chester's father, William Thompson, had also suffered unspecified health and mental problems and was facing a serious financial decline.

William Thompson was aware that his son had issues, but perhaps did not comprehend the depth of Chester's obsession with Charlotte. In May 1906, Chester showed up at the door of a Reverend W. D. Simonds, who did not know him, and confided in him that he was desperately in love and could not stop thinking about the girl. He told Simonds that he was "losing control of himself and feared the loss of his mind."[1]

A few months later, Chester heard a rumor that Charlotte had returned home from school. On July 6, a Friday, he ran into a mutual friend, another young lady who had also been away at school. He asked her if Charlotte was really back in town or whether he had "imagined" it. The girl confirmed that it was true, and that Charlotte would be "entertaining" the following afternoon. Later, Chester phoned the same girl to ask her if she thought he ought to send Charlotte some sweet peas or some other type of flower. The girl told him any kind of flower would be fine. Twice more, he phoned the girl to ask questions about Charlotte. By the third phone call, the girl was fed up and refused to speak to him. Chester sent a basket of sweet peas to Charlotte's home.

What the girl, and others, including Charlotte's family, did not know was that Chester believed Charlotte was in love with him, but her disapproving family kept her away from him. He believed the family had sent her away to separate the two love birds. What is not clear is to what extent Charlotte had been communicating with Chester, if at all, although it was obvious that Charlotte did not share his amorous feelings.

Regardless of Charlotte's actual feelings, Chester harbored other convictions that should have alarmed those around him or might have if they had known about them. Chester had told at least one family member that he believed he was being followed and persecuted by two mysterious men. The aim of these tormenters was to keep him away from Charlotte.

That Friday night, Chester walked to the Whittlesey home and sat on the stone steps of the grocery store across the street. He stayed there the entire night, watching the house. At one point, he believed he saw Charlotte come to her window and laugh at him. The next day, Chester went out and purchased a revolver.

On that day, Saturday, July 7, Chester learned that Charlotte was visiting the home of her aunt and uncle, George and Josephine Emory. George Meade Emory was a prominent Seattle attorney and judge, thirty-seven years old. He had practiced law in Seattle for many years with Bausman, Kelleher & Emory, had served as King County assistant prosecuting attorney, and in 1901 was appointed by Governor Rogers to the superior court bench. He had presided over the infamous William Meredith case. He and Josephine had six children, ranging in ages from eight months to eight years. Charlotte Whittlesey was the daughter of Josephine's sister, Louisiana (*née* DeWolfe).

On Saturday evening at dinner time, Chester phoned the Emory home, asking to speak to Charlotte. Charlotte came to the phone and Chester asked her if he could call on her. She said "no," that she was going out that evening. Before ending the conversation, she also told him that she did not welcome his attentions.

A short time later, Chester phoned the Emory house again. Charlotte, knowing it was probably Chester, asked her uncle to answer the phone. George Emory told Chester that Charlotte did not want him coming around the house or continuing his efforts to see her. In a bitter tone, Chester replied, "Oh, no, you do not want me to come to see her, eh?"[2]

At about 9 p.m., an hour after the second phone call, the Emorys and some friends, Mr. and Mrs. Keith, were taking the evening air on the front verandah. Charlotte had gone out. Suddenly, Chester appeared on the street and ran straight up the steps. He pushed past the people on the verandah and charged into the house. He was wearing a holster and a revolver. He entered the front hall. George Emory jumped up and followed him into the house. Chester turned and shot him. He fired two more times, filling the hall with smoke.

Outside, Mrs. Keith and Josephine Emory felt a bullet whiz by close to their faces. Mrs. Keith fell off the verandah and stayed there, too terrified to move. Josephine screamed and ran next door for help. Mr. Keith ran into the hall. Just inside, he tripped over the prone judge and fell. The smoke was so thick he could hardly see. He asked George if he was hurt; he was lying face down and Keith rolled him over. Seeing blood on George's chest, he tore open his shirt and saw a great chest wound. George whispered that the shooter had run upstairs.

Keith followed Chester to where the young man had barricaded himself in the children's nursery. The two youngest Emory children, Thomas, three, and Laura, eight months, were sleeping there. Keith spoke to Chester through the door. He told him the judge was not "badly hurt." He reassured Chester the family wanted to keep the incident quiet and that there would be no repercussions as long as he did not hurt the children. He described what happened next:

Just about this time the children began crying, and in my extreme anxiety I told the defendant that if he so much as harmed one hair of the children's heads he would be flayed alive.

Despite everything I said, however, the defendant refused to come out and he repeatedly reiterated that if I attempted to come into the room he would kill me and the children. His tone convinced me he meant what he said. He said he did not believe that he would not be harmed if he came out, and said that he could easily hear through the open nursery window the angry cries of those who had surrounded the house after the shooting.[3]

Indeed, having heard the gunshots and screams, a throng of neighbors had gathered outside the house. Meanwhile, Josephine had gone to the drugstore to find a doctor. When she returned and found her husband bleeding but still alive on the floor, George Emory told his wife he did not want her seeing him like this.

While medics took George Emory to the hospital, Captain Ward of the Seattle P.D. arrived and took charge of the hostage crisis. He headed upstairs and tried to force the door of the nursery open. Again, Chester threatened to shoot. At an impasse with the shooter and frantic about the small children, they called Chester's father.

Two hours after the shooting, William Thompson arrived. He went upstairs and talked to his son through the door. Finally, he was able to convince his son to give up. Police disarmed and arrested Chester Thompson.

On Monday, July 9, 1906, Judge George Meade Emory died of his wounds. He had been shot twice: once in the hip and once in the chest. The latter wound had perforated his lungs and proved fatal. On his deathbed, he asked his law partner Daniel Kelleher to watch over his wife and six young children.

Emory's funeral was held at the family residence, attended by 200 prominent lawyers and members of the Elks and Loyal Legion. They cremated his body and buried his ashes at Lake View Cemetery in Seattle.

Meanwhile, Chester languished in jail. Right away, his father, the attorney, aired his son's mental incapacity, laying the groundwork for his defense by reason of insanity. Chester claimed that he couldn't remember the shooting. However, he did insist that when he was on the phone with the judge, he had heard Charlotte crying in the background.

Several months later, on October 25, 1906, Chester's mother, Mrs. Ida Thompson, died without ever having been told of her son's actions. Her death certificate indicates she died at age fifty-two of "brain disease." Officials escorted Chester from jail to say good-bye to her, but he reportedly showed no emotion when he viewed his mother's body.

Due to the massive attention the case received in Seattle, officials moved the trial to Tacoma. In mid-December, the court began seating a jury. This process became a lengthy business, as they encountered great difficulty finding enough prospective male jurors who could pass the numerous objections from both sides. Women were not allowed to serve on juries in Washington

State until 1911. Since the case involved the son of a prominent lawyer killing a prominent jurist, no fewer than seven attorneys were involved in the trial.

To the charges of first-degree murder, Chester Thompson pleaded not guilty by reason of insanity. William Thompson, heading up the defense, delivered an impassioned opening statement that lasted four hours and shocked many in the courtroom. What he told the court laid a considerable stigma not just on Chester but on their entire family. He described the numerous ancestors of his wife and himself that had suffered from varying degrees of insanity. He confessed that he and his wife were actually related (though distantly) and that both came from the same aberrant family tree. He listed aunts, uncles, cousins, and grandparents who had killed themselves or spent their lives in asylums. He talked about his own brother, who had died in an asylum at age thirty-nine without ever learning to read or write. He described himself and his wife as high strung, nervous, and emotional. He went on at great length about Chester's "uncanny hallucination" over Charlotte, and about the boy's lifetime of eccentricities and lethargy.

Spectators marveled that William Thompson would be so willing to taint his entire family's reputation in order to save Chester from hanging. Even his eldest son, Maurice Wycliffe Thompson, was clearly on board with the tactic, at considerable expense to himself. Maurice Thompson was a rapidly rising officer in the Washington National Guard, where, despite the scandal, he would eventually achieve the rank of brigadier general.

Although he was trying to make a case for it, Thompson's background was not all neurosis and bad nerves. As a young man, he had fought for the Confederacy and took part in Pickett's charge at Gettysburg. He was a poet of some note, and had authored many works, including "The High Tide at Gettysburg." He and his wife were both descendants of Revolutionary War hero, Major-General Henry "Light-Horse Harry" Lee and Robert E. Lee. Ironically, George Meade Emory was named for General George Meade, who had commanded the Union army against Lee at Gettysburg. Emory's father had served as Meade's *aide de camp*.

During his father's lengthy revelatory speech, Chester Thompson sat silent, his head hanging. He showed no apparent interest in what was happening in the courtroom. He would maintain this demeanor throughout the entire trial.

The prosecution built a case that Chester was not insane at the time of the shooting. He had planned ahead by purchasing the revolver and had stalked the Emory and Whittlesey homes beforehand, showing "deliberate and murderous intent."[4] Afterward, he had expressed no remorse.

The state also focused on the horror of the event, displaying in court a gruesome pile of Emory's bloody clothing. The widowed Josephine Emory made a powerful witness, describing the death of her beloved husband and father of her six children. Mr. and Mrs. Keith described the terror of the shooting. Officers testified about Chester's refusal to come out of the nursery. Emory's law partner, Daniel Kelleher, recounted Emory's deathbed description of Chester's attack, how

Chester had shot him as soon as he came in the door behind the boy. Doctors recounted Emory's injuries in horrific detail. Charlotte Whittlesey did not testify.

Prosecuting Attorney, John F. Miller, made a vigorous speech about Chester's intent, describing in a "voice which rang through the courtroom" the latter's behavior just before the shooting, saying that Chester was angry about Judge Emory telling him over the phone that Charlotte did not want to see him: "And right then, gentlemen of the jury, this defendant had murder in his heart!"[5]

Prosecutors called four insanity experts, who all declared Chester was sane. On December 18, 1906, the state rested its case. The defense had subpoenaed forty-nine witnesses to testify about Chester's crazy behavior. In addition to numerous family members, those describing odd encounters with Chester over the years included former tutors, doctors, dentists, schoolmates, teachers, and friends.

His instructors portrayed him as courteous and well-behaved but said he was an isolated boy who refused to engage in normal activities. He would not attend his high school graduation or his sister's wedding. Some described how he would develop a sudden hatred for no apparent reason and disengage from a relationship. His kindergarten teacher, who lived next door, had considered him a smart student. However, in later years, he refused to acknowledge her, behaving as though he resented her, though she had no idea why. She said he developed a "strange impediment in his walk, stayed out all night and sat for hours gazing out his bedroom window, whistling and singing."[6]

Several others mentioned his habit of singing and whistling. The Thompsons' gardener described Chester's whistling as "a tune that wasn't a tune at all. It was very disagreeable. It sounded more like the old poll parrot that they had around there more than anything else." At this comment, the courtroom erupted in laughter and it inspired the first and only sign of life from Chester during the trial—he also laughed.[7]

Chester's brother Oscar testified that Chester had been fine until he was stricken with scarlet fever at nine years old. After that, he was changed and began to withdraw. This became worse as he grew older and he began developing obsessions.

Several years before the shooting, he became fixated with his teeth, describing them as tusks. He told his dentist that he would be heading to New York and Paris to get the teeth fixed and that the famed socialite and philanthropist Helen Gould would be paying for it. Several witnesses mentioned Chester's preoccupation with Helen Gould and with Adelina Patti, a European opera star, both of whom he apparently believed had the secrets to eternal life. He had tried to get a loan from a stockbroker so he could go to New York and find Ms. Gould.

The family who had taken Chester camping to Lake Crescent, where he met Charlotte, said that Chester spent most of that trip lying in a hammock, refusing to engage with anyone except Charlotte.

A local tailor took the stand and described an episode in which Chester had come to his shop to be measured for a suit. The tailor told him to come back in four days to try it on. Chester reappeared fifteen minutes later, asking to try on the suit. He then proceeded to order several other suits, until the tailor finally called the father who cancelled all the orders.

A neighbor described seeing Chester on the night of the shooting, before he went to the Emory home. The neighbor said Chester "was at the back gate of the Thompson's yard, his head on his arms, haggard, tired and weary (per witness). He told his neighbor that 'men were trying to get Charlotte's letters and were persecuting him.'"[8]

Oscar Thompson testified that during a jail visit with his brother, Chester had confided in him about the two men who had been trying to keep him away from his sweetheart. He said the men were always outside his cell window laughing at him. According to Oscar, Chester's nights in his jail cell were plagued with the conviction that he could hear Charlotte crying to him. He said Chester had developed a rash all over his body.

A defense "alienist" took the stand and testified that Chester Thompson was paranoid and delusional at the time of the shooting, disagreeing with the others called by the prosecution. The defense rested on January 12, at which time the prosecution presented several rebuttal witnesses. A young lady, Olive Vosswinkel, testified that she had known Chester for years. She said he was a normal boy, just bashful, that he had danced with her and other young ladies at parties, had shown her his poetry and talked about Charlotte. She said she did not see anything unusual with his obsession over Charlotte because Chester was not the only one. She knew of four or five others who were just as much in love with Charlotte as Chester was.

Chester's jailers testified they had not witnessed any peculiar acts and said he was eating normally with the other inmates. A fellow prisoner gave a similar testimony. A worker at the Piedmont Hotel at Lake Crescent remembered Chester from the outing in 1902. He contradicted the testimony of the host family about Chester's behavior on the trip, describing him as an "ordinary guest, dining at the table with the others, eating the same food, partaking in the same games, and taking numerous fishing trips." He disagreed with the host's statement that Chester had only eaten from a private box of health foods.[9]

Dr. W. T. Williamson, testifying for the prosecution, said he had examined Chester and found him sane. Chester had told him stories of fairies playing in the park, and that Chester and Charlotte would watch the fairies together. He said that Chester was shamming. He described this exchange with Chester:

> "Did you not know that it was not right to kill Judge Emory?" I asked him.
> "Yes," he said.
> "Don't you know that it is wrong to kill a man without provocation?"

"He gave me provocation!" he retorted. "He tried to prevent me from seeing someone I wanted to see!"[10]

On February 2, 1907, after almost two months, the case went to the jury. The verdict was returned quickly on the following day, after the jury deliberated for only five hours. They found Chester Thompson not guilty by reason of insanity. A great deal of consternation and activity arose. While the Thompson family thanked the jury, the Emory family learned of it while in their hotel room in Tacoma. The Whittleseys were with them.

Judge William H. Snell decided Chester's fate. Washington State did not have an asylum for the criminally insane, so there was some discussion about sending Chester to the penitentiary at Walla Walla. Obviously, William Thompson did not want his son in prison but rather in an asylum. However, Prosecuting Attorney Mackintosh quickly filed an information, saying Chester was too dangerous to be sent to an insane asylum. This was followed by a complaint filed by Maurice Thompson charging his brother with being insane and demanding he be sent to an asylum. Chester, meanwhile, remained in jail in Tacoma.

After much legal wrangling, in early May, the Washington State Supreme Court ruled that Judge Snell had the authority to send Chester to Walla Walla and that prison authorities would have to accommodate the special case. Within a day, Judge Snell did exactly that.

Still, it took more than a month to move Chester to the prison. In mid-June, he finally arrived and was promptly shaved and put into prison garb like any other inmate. However, this lasted only twenty-four hours. After a loud objection from William Thompson, prison officials quickly gave Chester back his clothes and he was hustled down to the hospital ward of the prison. He remained there for the next ten months.

In February 1908, William Thompson requested another hearing for his son, saying that Chester had recovered his sanity and should be released. He and Oscar Thompson had visited Chester and "declared him in perfect mental and physical health." The prison physician and warden supported his efforts. William declared that if released, Chester would go to Florida and work for a cousin's tobacco operation.

In May 1908, Chester's sanity hearing opened, this time back in King County. Unlike during his trial, Chester was attentive and chatted with those around him. He also testified on his own behalf. He said he could only remember going to the house and seeing people on the verandah. The next thing he recalled was smoke in the hallway and "a man rushing at him at whom he fired twice." He described his prison life and how he had recovered his sanity:

I now take an interest in things. When I first went to Walla Walla I tried to read, but could not understand anything I read. I kept trying and trying, however, and my mind got clearer and stronger. I suppose the process was like a man using his muscles, which grow stronger by exercise.[11]

In June 1908, less than two years after the shooting, the jury returned a verdict after deliberating for twenty-three minutes: Chester Thompson was sane; he was no longer a public menace and was safe to be at large. The state lost their appeal and within a month or two, Chester Thompson was a free man.

Thereafter, circumstances did not improve for the Thompsons. William Thompson's precarious finances had suffered even more from the strain of the two trials. Plans to send Chester to Florida did not work out and he was home living with his father in 1910, ostensibly working as a photographer. He also spent much of his time on a Wenatchee ranch that his father owned. In the summer of 1910, newspaper reports accused him of bothering Charlotte Whittlesey at a tennis tournament in Tacoma, but he defended himself saying he was only there in his new role as a photographer for the *Tacoma News*, a job that apparently did not last long.

May 1911 found twenty-six-year-old Chester Thompson unemployed and loitering around the home of another young lady, Miss Katherine Hemrich. Apparently, Chester had never met Katherine but had only seen her from a distance. She was the daughter of a wealthy brewer, Andrew Hemrich, who had recently passed away.

Over the weekend of May 20, Chester called on the residence, asking the widow Mrs. Hemrich if she wanted to subscribe to a book of his poems. After a brief discussion of his literary work, he asked her if he could take her daughter out. She replied that he certainly could not and asked him to leave.

On Sunday evening, Katherine's two brothers noticed that the notorious Chester Thompson was still lurking around the residence, and they called the police, who arrived and arrested him. William Thompson once again intervened and got Chester released. He sent Chester back out to his ranch in Wenatchee.

Meanwhile, others involved in the Chester Thompson drama had moved on with their lives. In October 1911, Charlotte Whittlesey married Walter Scott Fitz. Josephine Emory remarried to another lawyer, Charles Poe. At some point after her marriage, Josephine began receiving threatening letters. They were from Chester Thompson.

This time, William H. Thompson made no effort to clean up his son's mess. He committed Chester to the Medical Lake Institution, now known as Eastern State Hospital, near Spokane. This would become Chester's new home. Seven years after permanently committing his son to the asylum, William Thompson died.

Charlotte (Whittlesey) Fitz died in Seattle in 1936 at age forty-eight. Josephine (Emory) Poe had three more children with Charles Poe. She died in 1953 at the age of eighty. Chester Thompson spent the rest of his life at Eastern State Hospital. He died and was buried there in 1963.

Map of the Salish Sea. (*Courtesy of Stefan Freelan, the Spatial Institute, Huxley College of the Environment, WWU*)

Above left: Chief Leschi. (*University of Washington Libraries, Special Collections, NA1536*)

Above right: Isaac Ebey. (*University of Washington Libraries, Special Collections, POR2045*)

Home and blockhouse of Jacob and Sarah Ebey, parents of Isaac Ebey. (*Library of Congress Prints and Photographs Division Washington, D.C. 20540 USA*)

Crescent Bay. (*Photo by Roger Mosley*)

"Tomanawos board at the base of monument over 'Swell,' a Makah chief buried at Baadah Pt. Neah Bay W.T." Created by James Swan in 1861. Photo by Kathryn M. Stenzel. (*Courtesy Yale University Library, Beinecke Rare Book & Manuscript Library. Object ID 2003175*)

Freshwater Bay. (*Photo by Roger Mosley*)

The Colman house. (*Drawing by Richard Turner*)

Portrait of James Manning Colman. (*Courtesy of Gregory Manning Fawcett*)

Portrait of Clarissa Colman and daughter Clara. (*Courtesy of Gregory Manning Fawcett*)

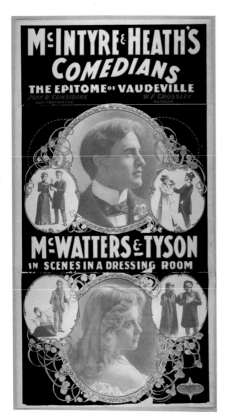

Above: Guy's Drugstore at left in 1901. (*Library of Congress Prints and Photographs Division Washington, D.C. 20540 USA*)

Left: The 1899 poster for "Scenes in a Dressing Room" at Considine's vaudeville house. (*Library of Congress Prints and Photographs Division Washington, D.C. 20540 USA*)

John Considine (left) and Carl J. Reiter, theatrical managers. (*University of Washington Libraries, Special Collections, JWS23106*)

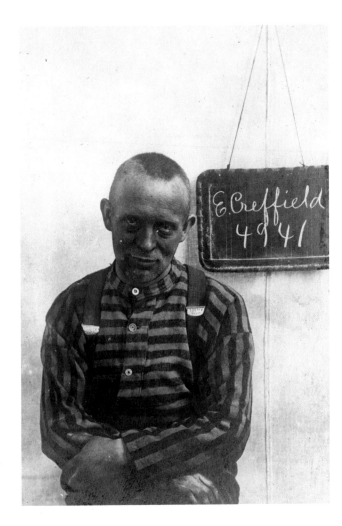

Left: Mugshot of
Edmund Creffield.
(*Oregon State Archives*)

Below: Mugshot
of Linda Hazzard.
(*Corrections
Department, Washington
State Penitentiary,
Commitment Registers
and Mug Shots,
1887–1946, Washington
State Archives, Digital
Archives*)

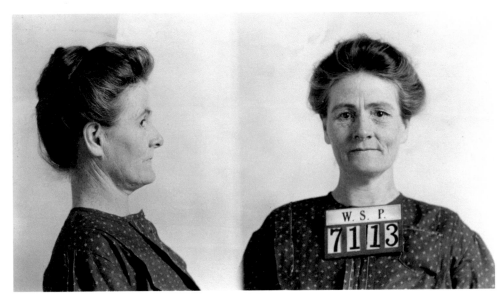

Milwaukee Hotel. (*Photo by Joe Mabel, Wikimedia Commons*)

Mugshot of Serafin Villaflor. (*Corrections Department, Washington State Penitentiary, Commitment Registers and Mug Shots, 1887–1946, Washington State Archives, Digital Archives*)

HIRAM C. GILL
1910 - 1911 ... REPUBLICAN
1914 - 1917 ... NON-PART: SAN

Left: Mayor Hiram Gill. (*Courtesy of the Seattle Municipal Archives.* ID 12278)

Below: Mugshot of Lee Oesear. (*Corrections Department, Washington State Penitentiary, Commitment Registers and Mug Shots, 1887–1946, Washington State Archives, Digital Archives*)

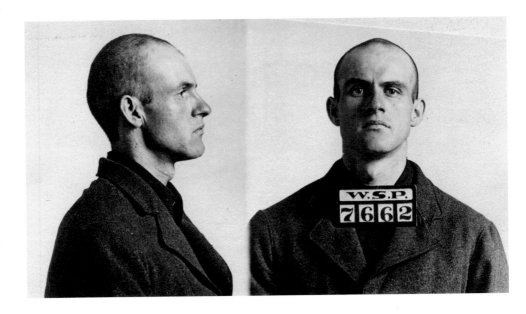

Bust of Logan Billingsley.
(*City of Anadarko/National
Hall of Fame for Famous
American Indians*)

Bust of Chief Seattle by
James Wehn. Photo by
Carol M. Highsmith.
(*Library of Congress Prints
and Photographs Division
Washington, D.C. 20540
USA*)

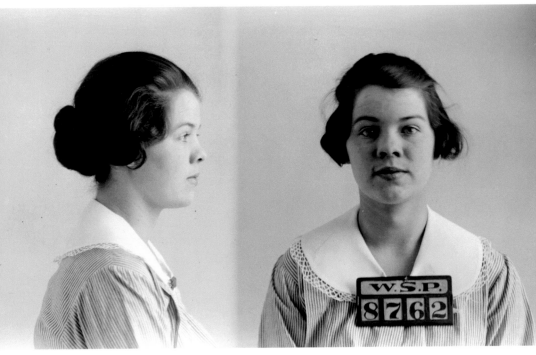

Mugshot of Ruth Garrison. (*Corrections Department, Washington State Penitentiary, Commitment Registers and Mug Shots, 1887–1946, Washington State Archives, Digital Archives*)

Mugshot of Douglas Storrs. (*Corrections Department, Washington State Penitentiary, Commitment Registers and Mug Shots, 1887–1946, Washington State Archives, Digital Archives*)

Mugshot of James Mahoney. (*Corrections Department, Washington State Penitentiary, Commitment Registers and Mug Shots, 1887–1946, Washington State Archives, Digital Archives*)

The Flieder house. (*Drawing by Richard Turner*)

Mugshot of Leo Hall. (*Corrections Department, Washington State Penitentiary, Commitment Registers and Mug Shots, 1887–1946, Washington State Archives, Digital Archives*)

Nine-year-old George Weyerhaeuser faces the press after his release. (*Courtesy of CriticalPast*)

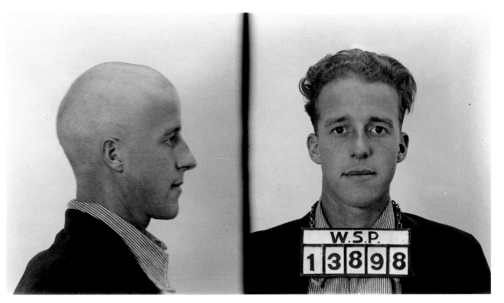

Harmon Waley. (*Corrections Department, Washington State Penitentiary, Commitment Registers and Mug Shots, 1887–1946, Washington State Archives, Digital Archives, http://digitalarchives.wa.gov, 7/15/19*)

Officials load the body of Charles Mattson into a hearse. (*Courtesy of CriticalPast*)

Lake Crescent Tavern. Photo probably taken around the time when Hallie Illingworth worked there. (*Library of Congress Prints and Photographs Division Washington, D.C. 20540 USA*)

Mugshot of Monty Ilingworth. (*Corrections Department, Washington State Penitentiary, Commitment Registers and Mug Shots, 1887–1946, Washington State Archives, Digital Archives*)

10

The Trunk at Alki Point
(1907)

The trunk lay lodged in the sand at Alki Point. Someone had bound it with a set of small ropes and it was heavy. Steffen Anderson and his friend thought it must contain something valuable, so they tore away the ropes and opened it.

Inside they found a layer of heavy rocks, which was strange. Beneath the rocks they encountered a quilt and a layer of soggy clothes. Steffen stuck his hand into the trunk, feeling around among the clothing. He found himself holding a shock of human hair.

It was Monday, September 23, 1907. Seattle police called to the scene were appalled to find the nude body of a small, young female—more a girl than a woman. Someone had gagged her with a hunk of blue material and tied a large handkerchief over her mouth. They had tied an undershirt around her neck with a great knot under her chin and strangled her. Other injuries showed that she had fought for her life. The killer had wrapped her body tightly in a quilt and weighed the trunk down with rocks, but it had not worked to sink the trunk. It had floated on the current and drifted to shore at Alki Point.

The body, and face in particular, was badly swollen from decomposition, but police noticed a small mole on her finger and a slight depression on the bridge of her nose. They fed these details to the press, hoping for help from the public in identifying her.

Among the clothing, they found a letter addressed to Edith Covington of St. Paul, Minnesota, written by her brother, Frank. As police hunted for Edith Covington, a brother and sister contacted them, saying the victim's description sounded like their missing niece, the recently married Agnes McCombs Covington. The pair, Jennie and George Robinson of Seattle, hurried to the morgue. Sure enough, the body in the trunk was seventeen-year-old Agnes Covington.

Agnes had been dead for several days. Her family told police that her husband was Frank Covington, a man in his mid-twenties who had married young Agnes only six months earlier. Agnes's aunt, uncle, and grandmother had objected strenuously to the marriage and had disowned her when she went through with it. Frank Covington had a bad reputation.

Police quickly descended on the Covingtons' room in the Keswick apartments at 916 Fifth Avenue, but the landlord told them the couple had moved out a few weeks earlier. Also missing was Charles Burlison (or Burilson), a friend of Frank Covington who had lived in the cramped apartment with the young couple.

The neighbors told police that the trio were constantly drinking and quarreling. They were secretive and did not like to use the front door of the rooming house, which would require them to walk up and down a hallway to their room. They usually came and went via the rear window to the apartment. If the landlord knocked on their door, they rarely answered it, and if they did, they opened it only a crack and never let visitors in.

Mrs. Mackay, the landlady, reported that Agnes was a "poor little thing," who always seemed to be drunk. Frank Covington was a whiskey salesman and apparently consumed much of his own product. Neighbors had frequently complained about rowdy episodes, and the Mackays had been trying to find a way to evict them.

The trio had moved out abruptly, without notice. A couple days later, Frank Covington returned alone to pick up some items left behind. He told the Mackays that he and the others were now camping. Frank was last seen about two and a half weeks before the trunk surfaced on the beach. The neighbors said they had not seen Agnes for a good week before that. In Frank's letter to his sister, which he had apparently left in the trunk by mistake, he said he wanted to go to Alaska.

Agnes McCombs had met Frank Covington through her grandmother. Although Agnes was living on her own at age sixteen and working as a waitress, she and her grandmother, Mrs. Robinson, were close. Agnes's mother had disappeared from the scene, perhaps through death, and her father was away "prospecting" in Okanogan.

Agnes and her grandmother had travelled to Portland together the year before, visiting a friend in that city named Mrs. Mitchell. Mrs. Mitchell socialized frequently with two of her tenants—Frank Covington and Charles Burlison. The two men had turned on the charm with their landlady's visitors and young Agnes was smitten.

Later, when the two men moved to Seattle, the first person they visited was Mrs. Robinson. Twenty-one-year-old Frank was soon romancing Agnes. Relations were all very friendly until the family learned that Frank was taking money from Agnes's wages as a waitress, and that he was mixed up with a woman from the "restricted district."

The tension came to a head one day when Frank Covington was visiting the Robinson home. Mrs. Robinson went into the kitchen, leaving Frank in the living room with the household cat on his lap. When she returned, she discovered him "torturing" her cat. It was unclear exactly what he was doing, but the episode was bad enough that Frank Covington was never again welcome in the Robinson household. This did not dissuade Agnes, however, and she soon married the man.

Another odd story soon surfaced, this one originating from the grandmother's friend in Portland, the former landlady. Mrs. Mitchell apparently enjoyed a drink or two herself, and she frequently joined in the festivities with Frank and Charles when they had roomed at her boarding house. One time, the idea came up that Frank, who had an effeminate appearance, ought to dress up as a woman. It would be fun, they decided, to see if Frank could fool their friends and neighbors.

So, a few nights later, Mrs. Mitchell loaned Frank some of her clothes and helped him put together a persona he dubbed "Mrs. Blank." After that, the two of them then went around Portland on a number of occasions, during which Mrs. Mitchell introduced "Mrs. Blank" to many of her friends and acquaintances. They were amused to discover that Mrs. Blank was "much sought after and admired by the men, who found her to possess such intimate little ways as are so pleasing to man in general."[1]

Their comical game soon got out of hand, however, when one of the gentlemen became so smitten with Mrs. Blank that he dropped to his knee, declared his ardent love for her, and proposed marriage. Mrs. Blank declined the proposal and within a few days, came clean, telling all of her admirers that she was actually Frank Covington and had just been having a bit of a laugh. The others were not laughing. A number of the dupes threatened to give Frank a thrashing.

It might have been around this time that Frank and Charles decided it was a good idea to get out of Portland. However, stories surfaced that Frank had resurrected Mrs. Blank once he settled in Seattle. It was not clear whether Agnes knew about these shenanigans.

Meanwhile, police could not locate Frank and Charles. Frank's employer, the liquor dealer J. J. Kelley, reported that Frank had vanished from his job, leaving behind his samples case. Some of Frank's co-workers reported that he often talked about problems with his wife. One time, he came into work with an injury on his head, claiming that his wife had hit him with a flatiron.

Charles Burlison worked as a steam fitter at the creosote works at Eagle Harbor on Bainbridge Island and his employer there also reported that he had gone missing.

Officers searched camping areas around Alki Point and found witnesses who said they had seen a couple engaged in a violent argument on the previous Sunday before the trunk was found. Based on Frank's comment in the letter, police wondered if Frank and Charles had fled to Alaska.

Intrepid reporters from the *Seattle Star* soon took it upon themselves to solve the mystery of where the men had gone. They interviewed folks from the rooming house on Fifth Avenue and reported every rumor that surfaced about the missing men. They learned from the Mackays that there had been a loud fight in the Covington apartment on September 1, a Sunday night. Neighbors were disturbed by Agnes's screaming and a lot of thumping around in the room. Mrs. Mackay knocked on the door of the apartment and the racket stopped. Frank opened the door enough to talk to her through the crack. He was wearing only an undershirt and trousers. He told Mrs. Mackay that Agnes had been drinking too much. Mrs. Mackey told him to keep her still. He promised he would, and that Agnes "will be still from now on." Mrs. Mackay said she had never seen Agnes again, and that the whole crew of them were gone entirely from the apartment by September 5 or 6. Mrs. Mackay also reported that Agnes had described herself as Charles Burlison's niece, though this was not true.

Other salacious rumors made their way into newspaper stories. One neighbor claimed that he had overheard Frank and Agnes arguing on the porch. Frank was trying to force Agnes to engage in intimate relations with Charles Burlison and Agnes was refusing. Another rumor came from an old friend of Agnes, who claimed that Agnes was actually in love with Charles rather than Frank.

Meanwhile, police located an expressman who provided a vital clue. Early in September, two men believed to be Frank and Charles had hired Bart McDonough to move a trunk. He was not sure of the exact date, but he said when that he arrived at the apartments, the men were waiting for him out on the sidewalk with the trunk. They were drinking whiskey.

He was worried about getting paid, so he insisted the men come with him. During the journey, they changed their mind about where they wanted to go. They ended up taking the trunk down to the steamer, *Florence K*, on the Galbraith dock. There, the three of them carried the trunk on board. He said he believed it was the same trunk that was found on Alki Beach. Detectives took McDonough to the dock where he identified the steamer *Florence K*, which traveled between Seattle and Eagle Harbor.

Later, police located a man who confirmed the story. The man knew Burlison and said he was on the *Florence K* with Burlison and Covington on a date in early September. He said he drank with them during the ride over to Bainbridge Island. He said he did not know what happened to the trunk, but that when they arrived, Covington had asked the way to Blakely.

A. E. Parker of Parker's Wharf, Eagle Harbor, said he remembered the trunk, saying they had unloaded it at his wharf. Parker's Wharf was private property, used for shipping gravel and sand, and Parker said it was extremely unusual for a trunk to be unloaded at his dock. The next morning, he said, he saw the tray of a trunk floating near the dock. Police speculated that the men had removed the tray so they could weigh down the trunk with rocks.

A local saloon reported that two young men looking like the fugitives came and purchased a flask of whiskey the same night. Others reported seeing Charles Burlison on the *Florence K* the next night, returning alone to Seattle.

Police were confident that one or both of the men had murdered Agnes, and that they had put her in the trunk. They confirmed that the quilt used to wrap Agnes had been stolen from the Keswick apartments. They said that the men had either dumped the trunk off the dock at Eagle Harbor or perhaps rowed it out into the Sound in a small boat. They told reporters that they were following up several leads and would soon locate the men.

Though stories abounded about Agnes being drunk all the time, the family stated that they believed Covington had forced the girl to drink liquor or perhaps had drugged her. Mrs. Mackay believed that Burlison was the nasty one of the two men and had probably murdered Agnes. She called Agnes a "sweet little woman" and said she felt sorry for her but did not know how to help her.

The Robinson family disagreed with that assessment, saying that Frank Covington had obviously killed Agnes because she threatened to leave him and expose his brutality. They said he had been boasting about his control over his young wife and bragged about doping her. They said he kept her boozed up on liquor all the time. Mrs. Robinson suspected he was hiding in Seattle under the guise of a woman.

The family also said that Burilson was a "thorough gentleman," and served as an older brother to Agnes. They said he protected Agnes from Frank. They explained Agnes's claim that he was her uncle was nothing more than a harmless joke, that he used to correct her for "little breaches of manners and street conduct" and so she began to call him uncle. The family insisted that Burlison could never have killed her.

Meanwhile, the family buried Agnes at Lake View Cemetery. Her father, Truman McCombs, sent a telegram saying he could not make it, but the rest of the family attended, along with numerous members of the waitresses' union.

As the days stretched into weeks without word of the fugitives, the governor and city officials offered a combined reward of $1,500. Numerous "sightings" flowed into the police station. One reliable report placed the men in Oakland, temporarily detained by police there for acting suspiciously. However, due to a telegram strike, Oakland police did not have proper descriptions of the fugitives and they released the men. Later, it emerged that one of the detained men had a "defective" eye, which fit the description of Burlison.

Another rumor put them on a steamship, the *Santa Clara*, headed for Alaska. The two men had reportedly changed their names and signed up to join a work crew in Katalla, Alaska. Authorities telegraphed their counterparts in Alaska and waited for a response. Reports in the press indicated that the Alaskan authorities were supposedly watching for the fugitives but failed to notify Seattle authorities, even after the *Santa Clara* arrived there. Later, it emerged that the men were not discovered on the *Santa Clara*.

In early October, Truman McCombs finally showed up in Seattle, "broken with sorrow," announcing that he would hunt down his daughter's killers.

A crew of sailors discovered a man believed to be Burlison floating in a small launch in the Strait of Juan de Fuca, exhausted and thirsty. His rescuers claimed that when he saw that they had identified him as Burlison, he jumped back into the launch and escaped.

A woman in Granite, Colorado, claimed that Covington and Burlison had burst into her remote cabin and forced her to feed them.

Closer to Seattle, a father and son cutting logs at Lake McAleer claimed they had happened upon two scraggly-looking men camping there. One of them had a cataract in his right eye. They were certain they had found Covington and Burlison and insisted that they would like to collect their $1,500 reward now, even though the men had disappeared.

In November, police received word that the fugitives were on the schooner *Henry Failing*, which had left Seattle on September 23 bound for Australia. Seattle authorities notified officials at Valparaiso, Chile, where the schooner was scheduled to stop for provisions on December 1. The men had booked passage as Jack Edwards and Arthur Hughes but matched the description of Covington and Burlison.

Chilean officials and the American consul there awaited the vessel, with extradition papers ready. However, it was not to be. When the *Henry Failing* arrived, local authorities interviewed them and released them.

Months later, during the following summer, more than a year after Agnes's murder, a member of the *Henry Failing*'s crew returned to Seattle. He said the authorities had examined the men in question. but they had "little trouble" answering questions satisfactorily and they were let go. He said the men "took off for the mines."

However, he said he believed the two men had been Covington and Burlison. He said they kept to themselves during the journey and that he overheard them arguing. He said the big one said to the little one, "I covered you long enough. If you don't do as I tell you, I'll give you up."[2] The sailor said the big fellow had a cataract in his right eye. This story was confirmed by a second crew member from the *Henry Failing*.

For fifteen years, nothing was heard of the fugitives. Then, on May 28, 1922, *The Oregonian* reported that the men had been found in Peru. Covington had disappeared, but local authorities were holding Charles Burlison in Callao, Peru.

He called himself Harry Ward but the owner of the American bar at Callao said he was known as Charlie Burlison. The man denied this and told authorities he had lost his passport. A week or two later, Peruvian police decided he was the wrong man and released him. Covington and Burlison were never caught.

11

The Deadly Fasting Cure (1911)

Disturbing stories about Linda Hazzard's "fasting cure" began appearing in local papers long before someone intervened to stop her. By then, almost a dozen of her patients had starved to death.

In January 1908, a ruckus arose in the household of Dr. and Mrs. D. D. Wheedon (or Whedon). Neighbors of the couple had complained to the Humane Society (which cared for humans at that time) that the dentist and his wife were starving their eight-month-old baby. The agency investigated and agreed that the baby was dying of starvation. When an agent arrived to take the baby away, Mrs. Wheedon pulled a gun. Somehow, reason prevailed, and the agent removed the baby. The mother was under the care of "Dr." Linda Hazzard.

Hazzard was an osteopath and dietician, although the status of her license was always under question. Police arrested her at one point for practicing without a license, though later a judge ordered the Washington State Board of Medical Examiners to issue her a license. They reluctantly did so.

She authored numerous books and pamphlets about fasting and enemas; the books are still available today. Pushing extreme fasting regimens on desperate patients, she claimed to cure a broad array of illnesses, including liver, kidney, heart and lung diseases. She kept patients on a diet of broth and water for periods between ten and seventy-five days. In one book, she wrote, "Death in the fast never results from deprivation of food, but is the inevitable consequence of vitality sapped to the last degree by organic imperfection."[1]

Her concern about "organic imperfection" was central to her program, and she exhorted her patients to continue fasting until their bodies were free of poisonous toxins, a condition apparently indicated by the appearance of the patient's tongue. She was also active in the Anti-Vaccination League, which met regularly in her Seattle offices. In 1908, they waged an unsuccessful campaign against the vaccination of school students.

The rescue of the Wheedon baby did not put an end to Hazzard's career. In June 1909, Mrs. Blanche Browning Tindall died of starvation. Twenty-five-year-old Blanche had been a patient of Hazzard's for a year. Her baby had also died under Hazzard's care. Blanche's distraught parents travelled to Seattle from Washington D.C. and demanded an investigation into the deaths, but nothing came of it.

The articles about Blanche's death produced another similar story. A prominent Seattle attorney, Oscar G. Heaton, told reporters and authorities that his wife, Viola, had died after fasting from March 23 until early May, under Hazzard's direction. He said he had been in shock since his wife's death, but the stories about Blanche had roused him. His wife had been troubled with indigestion and sought help from Hazzard. At the end, her system was so compromised that she could not even digest beef broth. Her death certificate said she had died of starvation.

Despite these cases, no one arrested or prosecuted Hazzard and she continued practicing. She later sued the distraught widower Heaton for payment of her fees of $50 per month (about $1,400 today), which he had refused to pay on the grounds that Hazzard had killed his wife. She lost the suit. However, the judge in the case pointed out that Hazzard's only fault in the case was that she had not insisted that Mrs. Heaton gradually reduce the amount she ate, as was prescribed in one of Hazzard's books. Mrs. Heaton had stopped eating all at once.

The following spring of 1910, Earl E. Erdman, a civil engineer for the City of Seattle, died of starvation after putting himself in the care of Hazzard. Earl kept a food diary of his treatment, which began February 1 and ended with his death on March 28. It shows he consumed only tomato broth, juice, and oranges in small amounts for two months. He complained repeatedly of headaches, abdominal pains, and trouble sleeping.

A couple of weeks later, a former Washington state representative, Lewis Rader, was dying of starvation in his room at the Outlook Hotel on Pike Street. The hotel proprietor, G. T. Olds, a friend of Lewis, became alarmed when he realized that Lewis had not eaten in almost a month and was half dead. Friends and officials visited the dying man, who was well-known in the region. Lewis insisted that Hazzard's methods would cure him of his stomach and liver troubles, and he refused to end his fast. His wife and son also supported his fast and defended Linda Hazzard.

A health department official, Dr. Frank Bourns, dug frantically through ordinances trying to find some legal way to intervene. He ended up filing an insanity charge against Lewis as a private citizen. When officials arrived to examine Lewis as part of the insanity proceeding, they could not find him. Hazzard had spirited Lewis out of the hotel and refused to say where he was.

In May 1910, after fasting for thirty-nine days, Lewis Rader died of starvation. Later, Hazzard would build her new fasting sanitarium at Olalla on property originally owned by Lewis Rader. It is not clear how Hazzard ended up with the property.

Yet another Hazzard patient, Maude L. Whitney, died in July of that year. Hazzard performed an autopsy and said she had died of pancreatitis.

Another year later, in May 1911, a prominent Seattle attorney, Frank H. Southard of the Morris, Shipley & Southard law firm, died at Providence Hospital. He had been under the care of Linda Hazzard for the second time. Originally, he had gone to Hazzard to lose weight and regain the athletic prowess he had enjoyed as a younger man. His health was good, but he wanted to get down from 225 pounds to 155. He lost 70 pounds but reportedly developed kidney trouble as a result of the extreme fast. He then went back to Hazzard to get help with the kidney trouble and she put him on the fast again. He died of uremic poisoning.

Other starved patients of Hazzard also died in 1911, including C. A. Harrison, the publisher of *Alaska-Yukon Magazine*; John Fluchs of the United Kingdom; and Stanley Wakelin, a New Zealand man who killed himself after a course of treatment from Hazzard.

However, it was another 1911 case that finally brought the law down on Hazzard. Claire and Dora Williamson were two wealthy sisters from England. They entered treatment with Hazzard in February 1911. Both were healthy women in their thirties, schooled in Switzerland, England, and France. They were well-travelled and had avoided targeting by fortune hunters more than once. Neither had married, reportedly because of their close relationship with each other. Except for an uncle in Portland, the rest of their immediate family was dead, and their closest companion was their governess, Margaret Conway, who was in Australia when they began the treatment.

Claire and Dora were extremely health conscious vegetarians who preferred natural treatments over "modern" medicine. Despite an apparent tendency toward hypochondria, they played tennis, swam in the ocean, and refused to wear corsets. The younger sister, Claire, was planning to become a kindergarten teacher.

During their initial meeting with Hazzard, the doctor performed no physical exam. She did not question them in detail, but still pronounced the condition of both sisters to be "quite serious." This, of course, worried the women, and they settled into a Seattle hotel, the Buena Vista, and began the treatment of tomato broth, two cups a day. This was accompanied by several vigorous walks, pummeling massage, and enemas.

The Williamsons assured each other they were feeling better, but both started fainting regularly, a condition that had never happened before. Soon, they both spent most of their time in bed, too weak to continue the walks. The weekly enemas got longer and longer, during which Hazzard required them to take a "knee chest position" in a bathtub so she could "flush" them out with six quarts of warm water. Hazzard started these sessions at half an hour each, then increased them to three hours and sometimes all day. Their neighbor at the Buena Vista hotel reported hearing them moan in agony. Soon, Dora weighed about 100 pounds and Claire 120. The neighbor said they looked worse than horrible, even repulsive.

Meanwhile, Hazzard told them they could not resume eating until their tongues looked clean and their breath was "sweet." Worried neighbors tried to get them to eat but the sisters did not want to disobey Hazzard.

Some reported that Hazzard was pressing the Williamsons about any "business matters" that might be troubling them. She wanted to know who was managing their money (they were themselves). Soon, she had the women dictating letters to bankers, though it is not clear what kind of account access the letters gave to Hazzard. Hazzard also eventually took possession of their valuables for safekeeping. One of their nurses, Nellie Sherman, grew worried enough to consult with a physician, Dr. Augusta Brewer. Brewer said to feed them at once but at that point the sisters would not take food.

On April 21, 1911, Hazzard brought two ambulances to the hotel to transport the sisters to her new clinic at Olalla, still being completed on the former Lewis Rader property. Neighbors at the hotel were shocked to see that Dora's face and hands were covered with white cotton bandages, with circles cut out for the eyes. It is not clear why she was covered with bandages, and the neighbors said she looked like a mummy. They also said "the mummy" could not weigh more than 70 pounds.

Once they were at the clinic, Claire apparently roused herself enough to became alarmed about their predicament. On April 30, she asked someone to telegram to their governess, Margaret Conway in Australia: "Come SS Marama May 8th, first class Claire."

When Margaret finally arrived toward the end of May, Linda Hazzard's husband, Sam, met her at the dock. He informed her that thirty-three-year-old Claire Williamson had died on May 19 and that thirty-seven-year-old Dora was hopelessly insane.

It took another seven weeks of a hellish cat-and-mouse game with the Hazzards for Margaret to get the half-dead Dora away from the sanitarium. Linda Hazzard had gotten herself appointed Dora's legal guardian based on her assertion that Dora was insane. She and Sam had also been trying, with limited success, to gain access to the women's bank accounts. Some $6,000 ($164 thousand in today's dollars) worth of jewelry had mysteriously vanished.

Finally, the loyal Margaret Conway succeeded in reaching the sisters' uncle, John Herbert of Portland, and the two of them finally moved Dora out of the sanitarium. It is not clear how Dora survived that long.

John Herbert was shocked when he learned of his niece's death. The sisters had not informed him of their plans to take treatment with Hazzard, as they knew he would not approve. Unfortunately, he had no idea of the danger they had been in.

Although Dora was now safe, she was still too weak to do or say anything. John Herbert recruited the help of C. E. Lucian Agassiz, the British Vice Consul, and they persuaded a judge to appoint Agassiz as the administrator of Claire's estate. They began preparations to sue Hazzard in a civil court. They wanted her indicted for murder as well and made their case to local authorities. Agassiz was also investigating the death of the Englishman, John Fluchs.

On Saturday, August 5, 1911, Deputy Sheriff George Posse of Kitsap County arrested Linda Hazzard and charged her with first degree murder. Since there was no jail in Kitsap County, the sheriff "incarcerated" her in a female deputy's home.

Hazzard defended herself vigorously, saying that she had always been persecuted by the "medical trust" for being a woman and having great success with her naturopathic cures. She could produce many patients for whom she had cured numerous ailments. Also, she insisted that the prosecution's star witness, Dora Williamson, was mentally incompetent.

The widower Oscar Heaton, still grieving his dead wife, offered his legal services to the prosecution, free of charge. John Herbert also sued Linda Hazzard for unlawful autopsy on Claire Williamson, desecration of a body, and theft of the jewelry, clothing and other items belonging to Claire. On August 8, Hazzard was released on $10,000 bail and her murder trial was set for October.

During the ensuing period, before the trial began, rumors circulated about Hazzard's prowess with "hypnotism" and "witchcraft." Once she was feeling better, Dora gave an interview in which she talked about Hazzard's psychological methods. She described how Hazzard had weakened Claire and her through starvation and how she manipulated them, making them question their own thinking. Psychological manipulation was still a novel concept for some, and one editor opined that what Dora really meant by "psychology" was "black magic," implying that Linda Hazzard was a witch. He insisted that Dora was making excuses for being a "woman of feeble intelligence and wavering will," and went on to decry the "coterie of more or less crazy women" involved in the Hazzard story.[2] The writer failed to mention the parade of prominent men who also starved themselves to death under the care of Linda Hazzard.

After a delay, Hazzard's trial began on Monday, January 15, 1912, in Port Orchard. By then, Dora Williamson had regained her strength and was ready to testify against the woman she now believed had murdered her beloved sister.

Curious onlookers had packed area hotels as well as the courtroom. Over ninety witnesses were slated to testify, many of them former patients of Linda Hazzard who had good stories to tell about their treatment with her. Hazzard had published pleas in various medical magazines asking for financial help and apparently got it. Counsel for the defense planned to call sixty-four witnesses, including three physicians who were proponents of the fasting or naturopathic method: Dr. E. Welden Young, Dr. J. Clinton McFadden, and Dr. Steven Olmstead. The state planned to call thirty witnesses.

The prosecutor gave his opening statement on January 19. He described how the lack of food had made the sisters too weak to resist Hazzard. By the time Hazzard moved them to Olalla, they were helpless. He said that Hazzard's lawyer, John Arthur, had shown up at the dock when the sisters were being moved. He entered Claire's ambulance and got her to add a codicil to her will giving Hazzard $125 annually. He also obtained orders to her banks telling them to release funds from the sisters' accounts to Hazzard.

As the trial got underway, the defense immediately moved to exclude Dora's testimony, claiming again that she was mentally unfit. The judge denied the motion.

John Herbert testified that his nieces had been in good health before they met Hazzard and that Dora was perfectly sane, with no history of mental illness. He described his alarm when he learned that Hazzard had gotten herself appointed Dora's guardian, and that the Hazzards refused to allow him to take Dora out of the clinic until he paid a settlement. Hazzard had given him an unsigned, typewritten letter, purportedly from Claire to him, testifying that she and Dora had entered the treatment of their own free will. The letter declared that if Claire died, it was because her death was inevitable. It was dated April 23, a month before Claire's death.

Dora Williamson testified at length about her experience. She said the nurses gave them either vegetable broth or fruit juice, never both in one day, plus eight quarts of warm water. She said her eyes began to hurt after the first week and she became confused. After some weeks, their broth included six asparagus tips. That lasted for two weeks, she said. Hazzard told them they had to continue the fasts until their tongues became "clean." She also testified about the prolonged enemas. Once they were at the sanitarium, Hazzard kept the sisters separated. Dora described the day when they came and told her that Claire was dying. They took her to Claire's room, and Claire whispered something to Dora, but she could not hear because Hazzard was talking through it. She described a moment when Hazzard pushed down on Claire's stomach, which made Claire pass out. Dora thought Claire had died at that point but learned later she had died a few hours later.

Esther Cameron, an eighteen-year-old nurse, testified for the prosecution. She had worked at Olalla briefly, from May 1 to May 15, caring for the sisters. She said Claire looked like a skeleton, with a large ulcer on her lower spine. Purple spots covered her body and she could not speak. Esther said she could feel Claire's backbone when she touched her abdomen, and that

Claire probably weighed 50 lb. She said a farm hand, Frank Lillie, gave Claire baths in the kitchen, and that Claire sometimes fainted during the bath. She described the tomato broth made from canned tomatoes and said that Hazzard told her to say it was made from fresh tomatoes. Esther left Olalla the Tuesday before Claire's death, which occurred on a Friday morning. Hazzard grew angry and fired her because she was sick one day.

Margaret Conway also took the stand. She denied that Dora was ever "mentally weak." She described her seven weeks at Olalla, sneaking extra food into Dora's meals, and trying to think of a way to get Dora out of there. As an employee, she was insecure about her authority. When she tried to pack up Dora's things to leave, Hazzard informed her that she, Hazzard, was Dora's guardian. It also turned out that Dora had signed a power of attorney to Sam Hazzard and supposedly gave him authority to draw money from her bank account. Finally, Margaret had gone to a local store and sent a cable to John Herbert. After he came, they succeeded in getting Dora out.

One of the Williamsons' bankers testified that Samuel Hazzard or the Hazzards' attorney, John Arthur, had demanded that Williamson funds be forwarded to Hazzard. They managed to get $1700 from this bank.

A physician, Dr. T. J. Baldwin, testified that the fast the sisters endured, of two months and twenty-one days, with only a cup of liquid food daily, would kill anyone. He said it did not matter if there were other ailments, as claimed by the Hazzards. He said Claire's death was likely hastened by the hot baths, enemas, and osteopathic treatments. He also said that in such a weakened state, they would easily be susceptible to any influence. The prosecution called other physicians who testified along the same lines.

The prosecution also showed pages from Claire's diary that had obviously not been written by Claire. In these entries, "Claire" described her great admiration and appreciation for Hazzard and indicated that she wanted Linda Hazzard to have her clothes and jewels. After a handwriting expert testified that the entries had been forged, the defense admitted that Hazzard had written them.

When the defense began their case, they called five witnesses the first day. Much of this testimony addressed the fact that Hazzard had been issued a license to practice osteopathy and fasting treatment, upon order of the court. Other witnesses declared that the dead body removed from the clinic had indeed been that of Claire's. Dora and Margaret had both stated more than once that they did not recognize Claire and called into question whether the corpse the nurses carried out of the clinic on an ironing board had been Claire's at all.

A nurse named Nellie Sherman testified for the defense, and said she was responsible for preparing and serving the food for the sisters. She said Hazzard did not restrict the amount of broth they got, and that Claire refused to take solid food. Nellie said she was told to give them whatever food they could assimilate. She denied previous testimony from a local grocer, who said

Nellie had confided that she was scared to death and "never had a case like this before and didn't want another."

She talked about how the Hazzards had loved Claire, and described the love, kindness, and tenderness the doctor had shown her patients. She said Claire had dictated the diary entries that Hazzard wrote. She said Claire also dictated the letters to the bank. She insisted that Dora was mentally unsound much of the time and that Claire often said she wanted to endow funds to the Hazzard institution.

Prosecutors interrupted her testimony, complaining that Hazzard was making signs to her. The judge told the bailiff to watch Hazzard carefully. Nellie refused to answer some of the questions and was evasive with others. Sometimes it took her fifteen minutes to answer a simple question.

Two farm hands who worked for Hazzard took the stand and denied they gave the sisters baths. They said they merely "helped" with their treatment. The prosecution accused one of the youths, Watson Webb, of traveling to Portland before the trial to bribe the nurse Esther Cameron, who had testified for the prosecution. He reportedly offered Esther four months' pay to ignore the summons and not testify.

Two other witnesses, local women associated with the Hazzards, testified that Esther Cameron, who had turned down the bribe, had a bad reputation. Another nurse, Sarah Robinson, who cared for the sisters for nineteen days, said that she had offered them cooked figs, tomato soup, spinach, asparagus, and cream. During her testimony, the prosecution once again complained that Hazzard was signaling the witness.

The defense then brought in an elderly man who testified that Hazzard's fasting cure had been beneficial to him. Hazzard's team had fifty others lined up with similar stories but the judge disallowed those because they were not expert witnesses. The three defense doctors testified, inexplicably, that Claire's death was not caused by starvation.

On February 2, the defense rested and closing arguments began. The defense declared again that Hazzard was merely being persecuted because she was a woman without a college degree and without traditional medical credentials that satisfied the "medical trust." The prosecution explained the difference between Hazzard's many patients who found the fasting cure beneficial and what she had done to the sisters. Hazzard had treated the sisters as normal patients at first, but once she learned about their great wealth, she "developed the criminal intent."

In his instructions to the jury, the judge gave them a choice among first degree murder, second degree murder, manslaughter, or acquittal. After twenty hours of deliberation, they returned with a verdict of manslaughter.

Hazzard immediately paid a bond of $10,000, pending her appeal, and after she left the building, she went in front of reporters with a "storm of denunciation" about her persecution at the hands of the medical profession.

The judge sentenced Hazzard to a term of two to twenty years hard labor at Walla Walla, but she was still free on bail pending her appeal. Meanwhile, she continued treating patients at her clinic in Olalla. She also began a thirty-day fast herself, whose progress was featured frequently in the press. Reporters accepted invitations to watch her going on horseback rides, designed to demonstrate how fasting did not weaken the body. She began giving lectures to the public, exploiting the newfound fame that had come with the trial. She announced she was working on a book and boasted that she had received an encouraging letter from famed muckraking author, Upton Sinclair. In July 1912, the State Medical Board revoked her license. However, she declared that telling people to abstain from food was not illegal and continued her practice.

On March 24, 1913, Mrs. Ida J. Anderson, thirty-seven, died while receiving the fasting cure under the care of Linda Hazzard. The coroner's certificate said Mrs. Anderson had died of neglect and starvation. Mr. Anderson, the husband, told reporters that he knew of a one-year-old baby who had starved as well. Around that time, another patient, Mary T. Bailey, also died of starvation at the sanitarium.

On August 13, 1913, the supreme court affirmed Hazzard's sentence. She appealed again. Meanwhile, under the care of one of Hazzard's "students," Fred Ebbeson died at the hospital after fasting for forty-nine days.

Once again, Hazzard's appeal was denied. Shortly after Christmas 1913, over two and a half years after Claire Williamson's death, Linda Hazzard went to Walla Walla. She served two years in prison, the minimum sentence for manslaughter, and was paroled on December 18, 1915.

Her supporters put together a petition to get her a pardon, which the governor issued on the condition that she leave the state. She and Sam took a steamer to New Zealand in December 1916 and stayed there three years, where she continued her "fasting cure" practice. There, authorities reportedly charged her with practicing without a license.

The Hazzards returned in September 1919 to Washington State. It is not clear whether the governor rescinded her pardon. After that, Hazzard reconfigured her operation as a "diet school." In the 1930s, police arrested her again for practicing medicine without a license. Around that time, her clinic in Olalla burned down. On June 24, 1938, Linda Hazzard, age seventy, died of starvation while fasting.

Meanwhile, after the trial, Dora Williamson had been swamped with marriage proposals, mostly from strangers. One of them came from a wealthy friend in Australia, whom she accepted. She later traveled to Australia to marry him. Dora and Margaret never accepted that the corpse removed from the clinic at Olalla was that of Claire Williamson.

12

A Case of Cockeyed Justice (1914)

On Christmas night of 1914, Seattle patrolman E. Geiser was making his rounds through Seattle's Chinatown. As he passed the Milwaukee Hotel at Sixth Avenue and King Street, he heard someone inside the building crying out for help. He thought the voice was screaming about a fire, so he pulled a nearby fire alarm and rushed into the building.

Instead of a fire, he found thirty-nine-year-old merchant Quong Chew groaning on the floor in room 223 of the hotel. Chew was bleeding profusely from a head wound and had numerous other injuries. A large, bloody shoe brush lay on the floor nearby. Although Geiser had not seen anyone running away as he entered the hotel, Quong Chew's attacker had escaped.

Chew was taken to the city hospital, where he managed to name one of the people who had hurt him, a white woman named Mrs. Lucile Goldy.

Police canvassing the area found a witness who was staying at the hotel. He reported seeing Mrs. Goldy and later another man rush down the back stairs and out through the hotel's Milwaukee café. This witness knew Mrs. Goldy by sight and had seen her before at the café. Another witness said the pair had come into his drugstore and called for a taxi. Police located the taxi driver, who gave them an address.

Three hours after the attack, police found twenty-year-old Lucile Goldy at a rooming house, where she was holed up with her husband, Vernon Goldy. Also in the room was a twenty-four-year-old Canadian who had been staying with the couple named Lee Oesear. After searching the room, police discovered a clump of blood-stained clothing. They arrested all three.

Based on interviews with their prisoners, police set out to find a fourth suspect, a nineteen-year-old Filipino man, Serafin Villaflor. They found him at another cheap downtown hotel and arrested him. Meanwhile, Quong Chew, having given police the information they needed to track down his attackers, died in the hospital.

Lucile Goldy quickly became a cooperating witness in the case, playing down her own role and pointing the finger at her accomplices. When she appeared in court several months later, reporters in the courtroom described her in glowing terms, saying she was "neatly dressed and her curly yellow hair smartly showing under her hat." She also behaved with "good grace and smiled pleasantly."[1]

Originally from Ohio, she had moved to Seattle about five years earlier. She had married Vernon Goldy eighteen months before in Shelton. Vernon had once stood trial for a "white slave charge," for which he was acquitted.

Lucille said she had only known Lee Oesear and Serafin Villaflor for a couple of weeks. Vernon had met Lee at a pool hall, where Lee told him his troubles, including the fact that he had nowhere to sleep that night. Vernon invited Lee to sleep on their sofa at the Medford Hotel where he and Lucile lived.

On Christmas night, Vernon had gone out by himself to a show at the Pantages theater, the popular vaudeville house run by John Considine. Lucile, left behind for unknown reasons, went out with Lee and Serafin. The trio migrated to Serafin's room at the Milwaukee Hotel, where they groused about how badly they needed money. According to Lucile, Serafin came up with a scheme to rob someone. They would find a victim who looked well-to-do and lure him into a hotel room with a promise of female favors. The men would bash the hapless victim on the head and take his money. They discussed what sort of head-bashing weapon they would use. It would be good if they had a blackjack, but they could not afford that. They discussed using a beer bottle or block of wood. In the end, Serafin found an oversized shoe brush with a wooden handle.

It was after midnight when Lee and Lucille went downstairs to the lobby of the Milwaukee Hotel and rented room 223. Serafin headed out into the night to hunt for a victim. He found Quong Chew, who reportedly was known to carry large amounts of cash. Serafin told Chew that a girl wanted to see him in room 223 of the Milwaukee. It is not clear what Chew thought it was about, but he went with Serafin into the hotel.

According to Lucile Goldy, when Chew arrived with Serafin, Chew said to her: "What do you want to see me for?" She replied that she had not sent for him.

Serafin then suggested to Chew, "You're here now; you might as well spend some money." Serafin then left.[2] Lee, meanwhile, was hiding in the closet. Lucile apparently undressed and climbed into bed, at which point, Lee burst out of the closet. The mugging did not go as planned. Chew fought back. While the men battled, Lucille jumped out of bed and into her clothes. She later testified:

When I left Oesear was kicking the Chinaman in the head … I hurried downstairs and left through the Milwaukee café. Just before I left Oesear wanted to put his hands on me. HE WAS ALL BLOODY. His hands were bloody. I said to him: "Take your dirty hands off me."[3]

Outside, she encountered Serafin, who demanded his share of the money. She said she did not have it. She went into the drugstore to call a taxi and Serafin followed her. He asked for money again and she gave him $2.50, after which he left. It is not clear if she had taken any money from Chew. She described what happened next:

About two hours later, Oesear came in. He was all covered with blood. He had Quong Chew's hat. He wore a red sweater, with a white band. The band was almost as red as the rest of the sweater. He put on Mr. Goldy's overalls.

He took out a silk handkerchief. It had a bunch of keys in it and money—about $26. Oesear said he wouldn't have bothered hitting the Chinaman for so small an amount. He didn't know the Chinaman was dead then. The money was put in a sack of fruit in the cupboard.

About an hour later, the officers came and arrested us.[4]

Authorities scheduled murder trials for all three. Lee Oesear, the man who had actually murdered Quong Chew, avoided trial by pleading guilty to second degree murder. He was sentenced to ten to fifteen years.

Serafin Villaflor went on trial in early March, during which Lucile Goldy testified at length against him. Villaflor testified on his own behalf for an entire day, denying that he brought Quong Chew to the room. He pointed out that he was several blocks away when Quong Chew was killed. He claimed Goldy was trying to get a lighter sentence by blaming him. Several character witnesses testified on his behalf. On the following day, the jury deliberated for three hours before returning their verdict: guilty of first-degree murder. The judge sentenced him to life in prison.

Although Lucile Goldy's attorney filed a plea of not guilty due to "mental irresponsibility," she denied that she had approved this plea and declared that she was perfectly sane. Her trial was scheduled to start immediately after Serafin's, but like Lee, she avoided trial and pleaded guilty to manslaughter. The judge gave her a one-year suspended sentence and sent her home.

13

The Brazen Billingsleys (1916)

On a warm summer evening in 1916, two Seattle police officers got off work from twelve-hour shifts. Sergeant John. F. Weedin and Officer Robert R. Wiley then headed to a friend's boarding house for a social gathering. Later, they agreed to drive a group of five women home to the university district. The group piled into a car at around 10:30 p.m. As they drove along Westlake Avenue, two dark figures ran out into the street and waved them down.

Wiley was at the wheel and he pulled over. The two men screamed that they had just been attacked by a Japanese man with a gun, then they rushed off into the night. Despite the protests of his frightened passengers, Wiley got out of the car. He pulled out his gun and walked across the road toward a warehouse. Weedin moved over behind the wheel of the car.

Multiple gunshots rang out. Terrified, the women jumped out and scattered while Weedin rushed to start the car. Tires squealed as he backed up toward the warehouse, looking for Wiley. Out of the darkness, another figure appeared waving a gun. He ran straight up to the car and shot Weedin in the head.

The gun fight at 2128 Westlake Avenue shook Seattle to its core. It would take years to untangle the intrigues, schemes, fabrications, and booby-traps concocted by those involved in the tragedy, and the lives lost that night would soon be forgotten in the political battles to come.

When police arrived at the scene that July 24, they found three gunshot victims. Sergeant Weedin, slumped at the wheel of the car, was dead. Officer Wiley had been shot in the groin but was still alive. A third man, later identified as Ichibe Suehiro, had multiple gunshot wounds. He was also alive. Medics rushed both to the hospital.

Wiley was gravely injured but still managed to describe what happened:

> I jumped out of the auto and went over to the place they pointed out. I
> found a Japanese there, standing outside the Billingsley warehouse.
>
> I showed my star and said, "You got a gun. What's the matter, Charley?
> What are you doing here?"
>
> Then he shot and hit me. I emptied my gun at him. Weedin was sitting in
> the car, and backed it toward us the minute he heard the shooting.
>
> I ran over toward him and so did the Jap. The Jap fired once, and Weedin
> dropped down over the wheel. The Jap fell then, too. Then a crowd began to
> gather and I was hustled to the hospital.[1]

Suehiro tried to speak but his English was rudimentary, and he could only
answer a few questions. He said his boss, Logan Billingsley, had given him the
gun. He said he thought the officers were robbers, and that someone had been
trying to break into the warehouse just before they arrived. Police called for a
Japanese interpreter, but before the person arrived, Suehiro died.

Police searched unsuccessfully for the two men who had been running away
in the street. Later, they discovered a chisel and two files in a nearby vacant
lot. They also found marks on the window of the warehouse that Suehiro
was guarding. They concluded that the two men were probably burglars that
Suehiro had caught trying to break into the warehouse. Suehiro had mistaken
the officers for the burglars and had over-reacted.

It soon emerged that the warehouse was owned by the Billingsley brothers,
well-known bootleggers with impressive arrest records in Washington State,
Oklahoma, and Virginia. Six months before, Washington State had enacted
a partial prohibition against alcohol. The new state law allowed only liquor
manufactured out of state. Those with a permit could import up to two
quarts of hard liquor or twelve quarts of beer every twenty days. The law also
allowed the use of "medicinal alcohol." In no time, the city had experienced an
explosion of "drugstores" that sold medicinal alcohol by prescription. Booze
was suddenly good medicine for all sorts of ailments, including depression,
cancer, and indigestion.

It was an open secret that most of the new drugstores also sold bootleg
liquor. Although the law had just taken effect December 31, 1915, the bootleg
market was already thriving. Not just drugstores, but soda stands, restaurants,
and speakeasies secretly peddled liquor. Hidden distilleries sprouted, and
those with enough capital brought in huge shipments from California and
other sources out of state.

Among the most prolific Seattle bootleggers were the Billingsleys. Headed
by thirty-four-year-old Logan Billingsley, other family members were Fred,
age twenty-three, Ora, age twenty-five, Sherman, age nineteen, and their

father, Robert W. Billingsley, age fifty-one. Ora claimed to be a tailor, but the others referred to themselves as "druggists."

It turned out that police had been watching the Billingsley warehouse for a couple of weeks. Logan already had a court date on a previous bootlegging charge. Patrolman Wilford Bayh of the "dry squad" had, in fact, searched the warehouse earlier on the day of the gun battle and arrested two Billingsley drivers who had a truck full of whiskey. Logan immediately bailed them out.

Mayor Hiram Gill was furious when he learned about the shooting. He told the police department to gather evidence connecting them to the gunfight and "get the Billingsleys." Police arrested the entire family, except for Sherman Billingsley, who went into hiding.

Logan denied involvement in the gun battle and denied giving Suehiro the gun. He admitted that Suehiro worked for him at one of his drugstores, the Day and Night drugstore, and that Suehiro had been sleeping at the warehouse. He said Suehiro had called him earlier to tell him he was concerned about break-ins.

Police broke into Suehiro's room where they discovered he had been diluting legal whisky by adding water and attaching government stamps to his "squirrel" product. They found paperwork showing he had worked for the Billingsleys for months. Some said that Suehiro was a "gunman," but authorities could not locate any reliable sources of information about him. Their efforts to find someone who knew him in the Japanese community went nowhere because the Japanese did not trust the police.

The day after the arrests, the *Seattle Star*'s "girl reporter," Cornelia Glass, interviewed Logan in jail. Logan enjoyed attention and was likely pleased when a large, fetching photo of him appeared on the newspaper's front page. Cornelia described Logan's southern drawl, his "air of gentility," and said he was a slight young man and very pale. He talked about his career in Oklahoma as "state manager" of the North American Life Insurance company, bragging about lush company banquets at the Astor House in New York City.

"That is all there is about me, I reckon," he went on, "except that I have been arrested several times for violating the liquor law. I do not understand this time why I am held. They tell me it's an open charge. If it is liquor violation again, I do not mind, but if they are trying to connect me with this murder it is a very different thing. Murder is serious."

When quizzed he said, "I do not think it wrong to sell any commodity for which there is an economic demand, as long as one does it honestly and frankly, treats everyone one right and pays his debts."

"I believe that many laws that are made by the courts are bad," he went on. "I think many man-made laws are better disregarded—most of them, in fact. Please do not misunderstand. I do not believe in lawlessness—" he shrugged his shoulders— "I find it rather difficult to say what I wish to say."[2]

He told her he had never married, which was a lie. He left out other notable details as well. He did not mention that he was still wanted in Oklahoma on liquor charges and that he had fled the state. He did not say that he had been forced to marry a young girl back in Anadarko, Oklahoma, after he got her pregnant. He did not talk about how he had abandoned his wife and their baby. He also neglected to mention that he had shot his wife's father and killed him.

Meanwhile, Mayor Gill met with members of the city council and declared that he would destroy the property of the Billingsleys and that he wanted relentless pressure on them until they left town. He wanted to make the town "too hot" for them.

While Logan Billingsley sat in jail waxing philosophical about liquor laws to Cornelia Glass, police raided his Day and Night drugstore at 1525 Third Avenue. They searched the place, removing whatever documents they could find. At the rear of the store, they discovered a trap door. Inside a secret compartment, they found evidence that liquor had been stored there. They soon found another secret cache under a stairway which contained two barrels of bootleg liquor. A third secret compartment contained more liquor.

After removing the evidence, officers brought in axes and "pulverized" the store. They smashed all the furnishings, the cash register, a typewriter, a marble soda fountain, all the showcases, and the mirrors. When they were finished, as a final touch, they sprinkled the ruins with some drugstore perfume called "'Wild Sweet Pea."

The Night and Day drugstore was not the only Billingsley establishment that police targeted in the aftermath of the shootings. They also destroyed the Billingsley's Stewart Street pharmacy, the warehouse, and a storeroom on Second Avenue. Finally, the Billingsleys obtained a court injunction against the city to stop the destruction.

Prosecutors charged Fred and Logan Billingsleys with first degree murder, saying they "did counsel, encourage, hire, command, and induce" Suehiro to murder Sergeant. Weedin. They did not charge Ora or Robert, the father, who were soon released. The court set bail for Fred and Logan at $10,000 each, which promptly arrived with their lawyer, prominent Seattle attorney George Vanderveer.

After paying his bail, Logan left the jailhouse. However, when Fred headed out, he was immediately re-arrested on new charges of forging liquor permits. Police then began hunting for Logan, whom they also wanted to re-arrest but had somehow missed him.

The new charges had to do with forty liquor permits that searchers had discovered in one of the drugstores. The permits, originally issued in the name of "Market Pharmacy," another Billingsley drugstore, had been modified with a clumsy new name, "Arket Pharmacy," and the forger had chemically removed the dates. Liquor importers could thus use the "new" permits to bring in more booze. Authorities declared they would ask for the maximum penalty for forgery of twenty years.

A rumor circulated that police had nabbed Logan, but he cheerfully called the *Seattle Star* and told them he was still at large. Authorities told attorney Vanderveer that every time he bailed out the Billingsleys, they would re-arrest them on different charges. In disgust, Vanderveer went into the station and retrieved the bail money he had paid.

Finally, the stalemate broke. Police released Fred and did not re-arrest him. Logan appeared the next day and was not re-arrested. Apparently, Mayor Gill was out of town on a fishing trip and had not left clear orders.

On Sunday night, July 31, dashing hopes that he could testify about the shooting, Officer Robert Wiley died. He was thirty-four. A hearing was held on August 10, during which numerous witnesses testified about the night of the gun battle. Not surprisingly, Judge Gordon dismissed the murder charges against Logan and Fred. The family still faced forgery and bootlegging charges.

Meanwhile, newspapers reported that the Billingsley books seized during the raids showed the Billingsleys were making $1,000 a day (about $23,000 in current dollars). After the judge dismissed the murder charges, the Billingsleys announced that they would give up bootlegging. Logan told reporters he planned to go back to college at University of Washington and finish his education. However, the entire story suddenly took a major shift when the Billingsleys announced they would sue the city for smashing up their property.

To the surprise and consternation of prosecutors, Mayor Gill abruptly held a meeting in his office with Logan Billingsley, where they discussed a "clean slate" for both sides. Logan said he would drop the lawsuit against the city. Mayor Gill agreed to drop all pending charges and stop the campaign against the Billingsleys. At the end of the meeting, Gill instructed an aide to fetch all the documents seized during the drugstore raids, and he handed them over to Logan.

In the months that followed, the city teemed with stories about the Billingsleys conducting business as usual. After beefing up their operations in Washington State, they expanded into Alaska, where some communities had banned alcohol. They used Seattle as a waystation, where Billingsley employees unloaded liquor off trains arriving from locations down the coast and transferred it onto ships headed north. Drugstores, now considered too hot, shut down, and mobile liquor stores appeared on the streets, where booze peddlers sold their wares out of the trunks of cars.

In late September, Logan complained loudly when prosecutors filed additional charges against him. He reminded them that the mayor had given him a clean slate. He paid a $500 bond, and in December, he fled to California.

That same month, a federal grand jury indicted Logan for bootlegging. Federal agents arrested him in San Francisco, where he had been living the high life at the elegant St. Francis hotel. The Feds indicted him for fraudulent use of the mails, conspiracy, and violation of interstate commerce laws.

United States District Attorney Clay Allen handled Logan's case. During their many lengthy interviews, Logan poured his heart out to D. A. Allen, confessing his leading role in a widespread operation that involved his brothers Ora and Fred. He implicated a transport service called Pielow Transfer Co., and another California operation called Jesse Hunt Moore Company. He admitted that his organization had transported more than $40,000 ($932,000 in 2018 dollars) worth of liquor, which they purchased in San Francisco and shipped to Seattle. They had "stretched" the liquor with water and other ingredients to a reported value of $200,000 ($4.6 million in 2018).

Despite this thriving operation, he fretted that he was almost broke, and his bank account had only $2,700 in it. Later, an intrepid reporter discovered that Logan was hiding $85,000 in a safety deposit vault in San Francisco.

Logan also alleged to D.A. Allen that he'd been paying off Seattle officials, specifically Mayor Hiram Gill, Chief of Police Charles F. Beckingham and several others, to protect him and his brothers. Logan said he had paid Gill $4,000 for the "clean slate" agreement and that his brothers had paid off Beckingham and the others. Gill and Beckingham vehemently denied the charges and requested a different federal prosecutor, saying that Clay Allen was biased against them.

On January 28, 1917, the Feds handed down indictments against Mayor Gill, Chief Beckingham, former sheriff Robert T. Hodge, four detectives, the Billingsleys, and others whom Logan had named.

After Gill's complaints about Clay Allen, the Feds appointed a special prosecutor, United States District Attorney Clarence L. Reams. Logan and his brothers, Ora and Fred, confessed to the federal charges. The Feds delayed sentencing for the Billingsleys while they built their case against Gill, Beckingham, and the four Seattle detectives, all accused of graft. The city officials all pleaded not guilty and the Feds set a trial date. They planned to use the Billingsleys as their star witnesses. Mayor Gill accused Logan Billingsley of orchestrating a frame-up.

The graft trial began March 8, 1917. The Feds tried all seven defendants together, and a crowd of defense lawyers appeared in court, each defendant having hired his own attorney. The most aggressive attorney, Walter N. Fulton representing Beckingham, soon made clear what the bulk of the defense would be—that the prosecution was relying on known liars and criminals to smear and defame respected public servants with long records in office.

During Logan's extensive testimony, Fulton grilled him about his illegal operations, his lying, and his vow to "get" Gill and Beckingham for destroying his property. Fulton repeatedly returned to the 1904 episode back in Oklahoma when Logan had shot his father-in-law and then later ran off to Canada "with a woman not his wife."

Logan defended himself over the Oklahoma murder charge. He told the court that when he was twenty years old, he had married eighteen-year-old Chloe Wheatley. He said Chloe's father had attacked his father and that he had shot his father-in-law to save the life of his own father. Oklahoma authorities had tried Logan several times for the murder. A jury eventually found him guilty and he went to prison on a four-year sentence. However, he was soon a free man running a bootleg operation in Anadarko. Police then arrested him and charged him with liquor violations, so he fled the state.

Fulton quizzed him about the whereabouts of his wife, Chloe. Logan said he and Chloe had divorced and that he did not know where she and their son, Glenn Billingsley, lived, but "possibly in Oklahoma City." Census records and Seattle city directories from the period indicate a wife "Chloe" living with Logan Billingsley but it is likely that this was not his actual former wife, Chloe, but other people using her name as a cover for living together unmarried.

Under relentless grilling from Fulton, Logan eventually told him, "I've begun to get disgusted with myself—but I'm not going to join a church." He also entertained the courtroom and annoyed defense attorneys by repeatedly saying, "I don't claim to be a young George Washington."[3] Logan also admitted that he had used as many as half a dozen aliases over the years, including "Clay Allen."

Gill's attorney, Frederick Bausman, also grilled him, questioning why Logan, who had never met Gill before, thought he could just walk into the mayor's office and offer a bribe. Logan implicated his own former attorney, George Vanderveer, saying that the latter had arranged the meeting in Gill's office and instructed him to pay off the mayor for "no less than $7,500." He boasted that he had gotten the bribe down to $4,000. He said he had carried a roll of bills half as big as his leg and had dropped it on Gill's desk. Citing attorney–client privilege, he refused to allow George Vanderveer to testify in the trial, so Vanderveer never addressed this charge.

Logan's description of the meeting in Gill's office contained inconsistencies. He contradicted himself about whether Beckingham was present and about who handed over the documents taken during the drugstore raids. He at first claimed that the mayor had told him that he had been "paying the wrong conductor," and later said that he had been the one to use the "conductor" metaphor.

He told the court that, prior to the "clean slate" agreement, he had paid a local Presbyterian minister, Dr. M. A. Matthews, $1,000 to lead a recall effort against Gill. Matthews had launched a successful recall against Gill some years earlier (Gill had since been re-elected) and was reportedly the driving force behind the current charges against the administration. It was not clear why Matthews would form an alliance with a bootlegger in order to oust a mayor he considered overly tolerant of bootleggers.

Logan also admitted he had paid a former *Seattle Times* reporter to write glowing articles about him and had bribed numerous witnesses to leave town rather than testify against him. Although he confessed he was a liar, he insisted he had never committed perjury. Fulton pointed out that he perjured himself when he used aliases to get liquor permits and druggist licenses.

During the course of the trial, the judge dismissed the charges against former sheriff Hodge for lack of evidence. Logan described paying off the four detectives—Meyer M. Peyser, John Poolman, James Doom, and Dan J. McLennan—to look the other way when he brought his liquor shipments through Seattle. Each received 50 cents per gallon of booze.

A witness corroborated this story, testifying that he had seen Logan apparently paying off Peyser. Logan had also told other witnesses who were on the take that the four detectives were "friendly." Attorneys representing the four detectives attempted to shift suspicion onto other officers, who by all accounts were clean and had been trying to rid the town of bootlegging. One ranking officer, Captain Charles Sullivan, testified for the prosecution, saying that he had protested when Gill handed the seized documents back to the Billingsleys. He had not supported the "clean slate agreement." However, a Billingsley employee testified for the defense, saying he had heard Logan on numerous occasions vowing to "frame up" Gill and Beckingham.

The trial lasted until the end of March. The lengthy testimony became a matter of witnesses testifying for and against the various players. The prosecution had no actual evidence. Stories of lies and payoffs abounded and created a tangled web of schemes and plots, many of which could be laid at the feet of Logan Billingsley, who meanwhile seemed to be enjoying himself.

The trial finally went to the jury on March 30, and the courtroom was a scene of great emotion and turmoil when the jury returned a verdict after thirteen hours of deliberation. Gill, Beckingham, and the four detectives were all found not guilty.

After the trial ended and things settled down a little in Seattle, authorities finally handed down sentences against the Billingsley brothers. Fred got six months and Ora thirty days, both in county jail. Logan got thirteen months at the federal penitentiary on McNeil Island. Attempts by Clay Allen to get a lighter sentence for Logan were unsuccessful, and Logan's new attorney filed an appeal.

On April 23, a Saturday, Logan was in a cell at a detention station in custody of a U.S. marshal. They were scheduled to transport him to McNeil Island on Monday. That night, Logan used a hack saw to cut through a bar in his cell window and squirmed through a seven-inch gap.

The news of his disappearance caused a great stir. He soon phoned reporters and promised to give himself up in a few days, but that he had to attend to some business first. A "few days" became a few weeks. On May 10, Logan finally gave himself up. Inexplicably, the court promptly released him on bond, pending his appeal. Meanwhile, he dictated a lively story of his escape for the *Seattle Star*, which appeared on the front page under his byline. He claimed that a mystery man had crept up outside his window and used a pole to hand him the saw, then vanished into the night.

While waiting for his appeal, Logan took off for Omaha, where police arrested him under the old Oklahoma warrants. He bonded out again and disappeared again. After the court denied his appeal, Seattle Sheriff Jack Stringer tracked him down in Detroit, where the Billingsley clan had once again set up a thriving bootleg business.

Finally, on July 23, 1918, authorities escorted Logan Billingsley to McNeil Island to serve his sentence. While Logan served his term, his younger brothers continued expanding their new operation in Detroit. The youngest boy, Sherman Billingsley, emerged as the "magnate" of the bootlegging world there. In October 1918, agents arrested the Billingsley brothers and charged them with importing over $200,000 worth of liquor into Detroit.

Logan served his full sentence and left McNeil Island on June 5, 1919. Seattle authorities met him at the gate and carted him off to the county stockade on the east shore of Lake Washington. There he would serve a three-month sentence for the old liquor charges that had sent him to exile in California. Oklahoma authorities waited in line, planning to nab him when the three months were up and bring him back to Oklahoma on the old bootlegging charges. However, on July 9, 1919, reportedly with Fred's help, Logan escaped the stockade.

A month later, authorities arrested him in Ohio. They contacted police in Washington, but Seattle officials declared that they never wanted to hear his name again. "Let Oklahoma have him," they said.

After all his adventures, Logan Billingsley appears to have spent the rest of his life rehabilitating himself. In 1920, he married a Miami woman, Frances Longworth, and they had three children: Jerome, Robert, and Francis. The family moved around a lot—they lived in Los Angeles, Alaska, Miami, and Cuba. In Havana, Logan ran an export/import business. Later, back in New York, he built the Theodore Roosevelt apartment building. By the time of his death in 1963, he was considered a civic leader and philanthropist. The Native American community in Oklahoma celebrated him for founding the

National Hall of Fame for Famous American Indians. He died in Oklahoma and is honored with a bust in Anadarko, Oklahoma.

Logan's first wife, Chloe, raised their son, Glenn, and eventually remarried to James Young. In 1941, Glenn Billingsley, the son of Logan and Chloe, married Barbara Combes. Barbara Billingsley, an actress, signed a contract with MGM in the mid-1940s and the couple moved to Los Angeles. While Glenn Billingsley ran a popular restaurant called Billingsley's Golden Bull, Barbara Billingsley became famous in the late 1950s when playing June Cleaver in the popular television show, *Leave it to Beaver*.

Fred Billingsley hit troubled waters in 1932 in Los Angeles when he shot and killed his doctor, named Rieger, who was a "prominent film colony physician." Fred was suffering from pneumonia and delirium and he was not charged. Newspapers described him as a wealthy retired oil man.

Sherman Billingsley became famous for operating a favorite celebrity hotspot, the Stork Club in New York City, where he rubbed elbows with the rich, famous and powerful. Sergeant Weedin, whose murder began the saga, was survived by a widow, four sons and four daughters. He was forty-six when he died. His wife later remarried to Ernest Lewis, a barber. Officer Robert Wiley left behind a wife, Ella, and a young son, Cole. Ichibe Suehiro does not appear in any census records for Seattle.

14

The Mystery of the Sculptor's Wife (1917)

Seattle's celebrated sculptor, James A. Wehn, later said he was not concerned when his wife, Florence, did not return home that Tuesday night. She had been at a birthday party at her parents' house and she sometimes stayed over with them.

This particular birthday party was especially important to the family. Florence's parents, Paul and Maggie Haubris, had recently lost their foster daughter to tuberculosis, and they were celebrating the birthday of her son, fifteen-year-old Julian Lindsay. It was the boy's first birthday without his mother.

James had not gone to the party with his wife. He was working on a commission at the University of Washington, creating a death mask for recently deceased Professor Emeritus Orson Bennett Johnson. That night he returned home late and stayed up to read until about 1 a.m. When Florence still had not returned home, he assumed she had stayed over, and he went to sleep.

The next morning, as he waited for his wife to return, a policeman showed up at his door asking about Florence. James assured the officer his wife should be at her parents' house, but that he could not phone them because he did not have a telephone. The officer left to call the Haubris house, leaving a patrolman with James.

When the officer returned, he broke the news: Florence did not stay over at her parents' house. That morning, a lad riding his bike had discovered Florence Wehn's body lying in a nearby gulch. She had been murdered.

James did not take the news well. He mumbled incoherently and seemed near collapse. Still, the officer took him to the site where they found her body, about two blocks away from their home. The area was isolated, with no houses and only a small corner light.

Twenty-seven-year-old Florence had fought her attacker. During the battle, the killer had smashed her in the temple, cut her hands, and broken her finger. Her things lay scattered in the grass, including her purse, a packet containing birthday cake, a rose cutting, and a bottle of milk. Her clothing seemed intact at first, but subsequent inspection by Deputy Coroner Koepfil indicated that "other" garments were torn. She had half a dozen undisclosed injuries on her body.

Florence was a pretty young woman who dressed well and worked as a telephone operator at the Pantorium Dye Works. She had worked there for six years, staying on after her marriage to James in 1915. They lived on modest means, and she wanted to support his career as an artist and sculptor.

James and Florence had been married for about two years and had only recently moved into their own home at 2214 12th Avenue. The couple had known each other since childhood and had attended school together. James Wehn's career had taken off since the unveiling of his celebrated statue of Chief Seattle in 1912, which still stands today at Tilikum Place on the corner of Denny and Fifth Avenues.

After leaving the scene of Florence's death, police escorted James down to the station for an interview. He said that he had last seen Florence the previous morning. She left the house in good spirits at 7:30 a.m.

Florence's grief-stricken parents provided a little more information about her movements that night. They had tried to convince her to spend the night, but she had insisted on heading home or "Jamie" might be worried about her. She left their home at about 10 p.m., aiming to take the streetcar. Maggie Haubris repeated her daughter's last words to her: "I'll see you again soon, mamma." The Haubrises were already reeling from the death of their foster daughter, and the murder of Florence devastated the family. Florence had just one younger brother, Paul S. Haubris, who was still in high school.

The family was further horrified when the coroner told them that the murderer had attacked Florence between 11 p.m. and 12 a.m., shortly after she got off the streetcar, but that she had died at around 4 a.m. Wednesday morning, April 18, 1917. Gravely injured, she had spent a long night in the dark gulch, slowly expiring.

A man who lived close to the scene on 12th Avenue said his windows had been open that night, but he heard no screams. This led detectives to question whether she might have been attacked elsewhere and dumped.

The streetcar conductor remembered Florence. She got off the car at 10th Avenue and West Wheeler at 11.30 p.m. He said a man got off the car at the same time but headed off in another direction. This same man boarded his car again shortly after midnight and returned downtown. The police started a search for the man.

Police were also investigating a second attack that occurred in another part of town. A man had jumped out of the bushes and attacked a young woman from behind. He dragged her into an abandoned house that had been gutted by fire. He bound and gagged her and was ripping at her clothes when he heard voices and ran off.

Meanwhile, police interrogated James Wehn and searched his home. James had told them that Florence often stayed over at her parents' house, but the Haubris family denied this. Police pressed him on the discrepancy, but his answers apparently satisfied them for the time being and they sent him home.

Investigators began working on a "Jack the Ripper" theory and issued warnings to women not to go anywhere unescorted at night. Another report came in of a man in a long, black coat and corduroy trousers, who was chasing girls at the Queen Anne high school. Police also followed up on a story about a man found in Port Ludlow in a "deranged mental condition" with blood on his clothes. However, the man provided a solid alibi.

Officials and experts could not agree on the motive for the attack. Some news reports referred to the killer as a "datist," which was described as "a sensual degenerate who 'inflicts injury and punishment upon the object of his affection.'"[1] The county coroner, Dr. Tiffin, made a thorough examination of Florence's body and announced that he found no evidence that the attacker had "accomplished a fiendish purpose." However, Captain Charles Tennant, chief of detectives, disagreed. "'It looks to me as though the woman's clothes had been tampered with,' he said, after making another examination today. 'But the coroner thinks not.'"[2]

On April 23, the Haubris family held a memorial service for Florence, but James did not attend. Finally, on May 2, 1917, the coroner held a formal inquest. It lasted all day, and fifteen witnesses testified.

The coroner described in detail the injuries he found on Florence's body: four head wounds, a bruise on her cheek, and two broken fingers. He identified a skull fracture behind her ear as the cause of death. The officer who had gone to James Wehn's home the morning Florence was discovered testified about James's reaction to his appearance at the door.

> Although I asked him several questions about his wife, he did not suspect that anything was wrong. I went away to call up Haubris by telephone, leaving Patrolman Ballard at the house. When I left, Wehn had asked absolutely no question as to what was the matter with his wife.[3]

James Wehn himself was the principal witness at the inquest. He answered questions about lights that neighbors had reported seeing in his house during the early morning hours of Wednesday, April 18. He said he had been up reading late and fell asleep, and that he had also left the porch light on for Florence. He awoke at 1 a.m. and turned out the lights.

A member of the coroner's jury asked why he hadn't attended her funeral. He answered:

> Florence and I had often talked about death, naturally, because it was a part of my business to make death masks for people here in Seattle. We had almost agreed not to attend each other's funeral, no matter which of us went first. I just couldn't go.[4]

When asked about his relationship with Florence, he "declared the relations between himself and Mrs. Wehn had always been most pleasant. 'We never quarreled,' he said."[5]

However, his father-in-law, Paul Haubris, contradicted this statement, perhaps revealing some doubt in his mind about James's innocence. Haubris, who worked as the night telephone operator for the Seattle Police Department, said that Florence and James had indeed quarreled:

> They had been estranged for a period of three years just before their marriage. Since then, Haubris did not know whether they had been altogether happy or not. He recalled the circumstances of his daughter's marriage with Wehn, which occurred unexpectedly in Port Orchard, where the couple had gone to spend a weekend with a friend of Mrs. Wehn's.[6]

Although the inquest lasted all day, very little new evidence emerged, and the case languished over the following months.

In a strange twist, in late May, James Wehn reported that someone burgled his house and took Florence's will from a bureau drawer. He was reportedly the sole beneficiary of Florence's estate, which included property valued at $3,000 (about $60,000 in current money).

Also in May, a Maple Valley woman was attacked, and police found the circumstances uncannily similar to the attack on Florence Wehn. The attacker had dragged Mrs. R. T. Hoag to a vacant lot, beat her, and left her. She had survived and was in the hospital in serious condition.

In July, a series of attacks created a siege mentality among the women of Seattle and the environs. An assailant the press dubbed "The Slugger" was going around bashing women on the head with a blunt instrument. "The Slugger" targeted women walking by themselves at night. He left the victims with serious injuries, including several fractured skulls. One victim reported that the attacker muttered at her to remember "what happened to the woman on Queen Anne Hill," an apparent reference to Florence.

The attacks occurred in different sections of the city— Queen Anne Hill, Rainier Valley, Madrona Park, Fauntleroy, and downtown. Inexplicably, police in Spokane and Victoria reported similar events.

In October, a seventeen-year-old girl named Ruth De Maritt was found dead near Seattle Golf and Country Club. Ruth had disappeared nearly two months earlier in August, last seen taking a streetcar. Someone had murdered her and dragged her into the brush on a rarely used path through the woods. Her head was no longer attached to her body, but police said this was likely due to decomposition or possibly depredation.

A report came in from Kitsap County, saying a woman's pit bull terrier had saved her by biting an attacker. A posse of 150 men was reportedly unable to apprehend another attacker in the university area of Seattle.

As the hysteria increased, police interviewed more than twenty suspects in the "Slugger" case, which they still believed could be related to the Wehn murder. Newspapers said many of the suspects were "suspicious foreigners." Numerous women reported being followed. Vigilantes told police about characters they considered questionable. Authorities appointed 100 special officers from a list of civilian volunteers.

Despite all the consternation, months went by and the "Slugger" headlines eventually disappeared. The attacks ceased and the vigilantes went home. The "Slugger" or "Sluggers" were never apprehended. The Florence Wehn case went cold and her murder has never been solved.

Meanwhile, James A. Wehn moved back into his parents' home. He foundered for several years, apparently grieving the violent death of his wife. After he delayed finishing several large commissions, he finally began to move on and resume his career.

Late in life, at age sixty-seven, James remarried to Lillian Hocking, a former student. He died in 1973 at the age of ninety-one.

As for the Haubris family, fate had one more shattering blow to deliver. Florence's younger brother, Paul S. Haubris, seventeen years old, enlisted in the coast artillery, then transferred to the Second Washington to fight in World War I. He was still a freshman at Broadway High School when he enlisted. On July 20, 1918, about a year and a half after his sister was murdered, Paul was killed in action. He is buried at the Aisne-Marne American Cemetery and Memorial in Belleau, France.

15

Murder in the Bon Marché Tearoom (1919)

To the casual observer, the scene at the Bon Marché tearoom might have looked charming—two neatly dressed young women deep in discussion, sharing a simple luncheon. However, the conversation was anything but simple, and what happened next would destroy many lives.

The younger of the two women, Ruth Garrison, was an eighteen-year-old high school dropout. She had invited the other, twenty-eight-year-old Grace Elizabeth Storrs, to have lunch and talk over their little problem: Ruth was having an affair with Grace's husband.

Seated at a nearby table, Grace's mother and sister monitored the situation. Grace had been apprehensive about the invitation and had asked them to come. Her instincts were sound. As they spooned bits of fruit cocktail from glass cups, Ruth went on the offense, demanding to know if Grace had heard from her husband.

What Grace did not know was that Ruth had, just the day before, returned from Okanogan where she had been staying in a hotel with Douglas "Dudley" Storrs, in the same room, in the same bed.

What Ruth did not know was that Douglas and Grace had been exchanging letters about how Douglas hoped to find a new rental home soon so Grace could join him in their new life.

Ruth told Grace that she planned to travel to Alaska with a friend for several months and that she would leave Douglas Storrs alone during that period. She said that she expected them to be divorced by the time she got back. Grace was just assuring Ruth that she would not divorce Douglas when she gasped and began convulsing.

Her mother and sister and others rushed to the table. Confused about what was happening, her sister begged her to stop, but Grace could not respond. Attendants carried Grace to the store's emergency hospital where nurses tried to help. Someone called an ambulance. The convulsions continued. By the time the ambulance arrived, Grace was dead. Dr. Charles C. Tiffin was brought in, and he declared that Grace Storrs had been poisoned.

Meanwhile, in the commotion, Ruth had disappeared. A frantic search for her ended when she emerged from the ladies' rest room "in complete possession of herself," according to one witness. While others milled around in a state of shock, Ruth went to the phone and called her aunt to come and pick her up, reportedly telling her she was "in trouble."

Later on, Dr. Tiffin went to talk to Ruth at her aunt's home. He was surprised to find the young woman asleep on the sofa. They awakened her and asked her to explain what happened. She told them that Grace Storrs must have committed suicide. Grace, she said, had made several attempts in the past to kill herself—with a gun, with gas, and with Lysol. She said that Douglas Storrs had told her these things about his wife.

She was frank about her relationship with "Dud." She loved him, she said. She admitted that she had stopped by a drugstore earlier in the day but couldn't remember where it was. Ruth went to the police station to answer questions. In the lobby of the station, she stopped to chat with eager reporters. Ruth said:

> I love Dudley M. Storrs—I want him ... But I don't know what killed his wife. I wanted to play square with her. That is why I asked her to lunch with me. That is why I told her I would go to Alaska and not write to him. But I wanted to know if she intended to divorce him.[1]

After an interview, the police allowed Ruth to go home to her aunt's house.

Dr. Tiffin suspected that Grace had died of strychnine poisoning and he arranged to have a *post-mortem* conducted by Professor William Dane from the chemistry department at University of Washington.   Back in Okanogan, where Douglas Storrs had relocated to a few months earlier, he received a telegram from Grace's father: "Grace died this afternoon while talking with Miss Garrison."[2] As word filtered across the state, reporters swarmed around Storrs. He confirmed what Ruth had said—that his wife had tried to kill herself before. He told them that this time she had succeeded.

The police saw it differently. The next morning, at 1:30 a.m., they arrived at the home of Mr. and Mrs. Esary, Ruth's aunt and uncle. They arrested Ruth Garrison for the murder by poison of Grace Storrs.

Ruth Garrison had not had much fun in her young life. Born in a crowded Virginia cabin and brought to Washington at age eight, she was the eleventh child of Joseph and Talitha Garrison. Her father was known as a gruff, bad-tempered man who worked in masonry and lumber. Some said the parents doted on her as the youngest child; others said the father beat her and the other Garrison children. As she approached her high school years, she convinced her parents to let her leave their home on Camano Island and move in with friends in Seattle so she could attend Queen Anne high school.

Before graduating, she left school to take a job in city offices downtown. It was there that she met a deputy sheriff named Douglas Storrs. Twenty-seven-year-old Storrs was a "rough and tumble" fellow who had married Grace Glatz two years earlier. A high school dropout, he worked as a mechanic and a driver for the sheriff's department.

His fellow workers said he spent a lot of time chatting with the cheerful young Ruth. He brought her candy and gave her a wristwatch. After a dispute over a raise, he quit the sheriff's office and took work at the shipyards. In January 1919, two months before his wife's death, he left Seattle for Okanogan. He often talked about making a fortune mining for gold in Siberia but apparently had made no move to head to that remote region.

Grace's parents told police that Douglas had been negligent about sending money to his wife and that she had moved back in with them. Grace's father said he did not believe his daughter had committed suicide; he figured she must have died of natural causes, that she simply fainted and did not wake up.

On the day of Ruth's arrest, Captain of Detectives Charles Tennant and Deputy Prosecuting Attorney John D. Carmody interviewed her at length. They confronted her with the results of the *post-mortem*, which found a fatal amount of strychnine in Grace's stomach. They also had a witness statement from a woman who had been eating lunch near Ruth's table. The witness noticed Ruth stirring the fruit cocktail before Grace arrived and saw Ruth push the glass cup across the table. Ruth then rose, looked around, and tipped the chair against the table in anticipation of her guest.

By late afternoon, cornered with this evidence, Ruth Garrison confessed. She told them exactly what she had done, in great detail. On Monday, she had returned from her visit with Douglas in Okanogan, where the pair had presented themselves as Mr. and Mrs. Storrs. During this trip, she had apparently relinquished her virginity to the man she loved. On Tuesday morning, she felt determined to do something about the stalemate with Grace, who had discovered the affair weeks earlier. She phoned Grace and asked her to lunch so they could talk things over.

Before the lunch meeting, she went into a drugstore and tried to purchase strychnine, explaining that she wanted it to kill cats. The druggist refused to sell it to her without a prescription. She tried and failed to find a doctor who would write a prescription for her. At a drugstore on Union Street, she found a druggist who sold her the strychnine. To cover her tracks, she signed the purchase slip Ruth Green at 3515 Summit Ave. She arrived at the Bon Marché tearoom before Grace and ordered the meal. A fruit cocktail arrived before Grace came in, and Ruth put ten cents worth of strychnine into Grace's cup.

The detectives asked her to take them to the place where she bought the strychnine. She led them to the Cut Rate Drugstore at 308 Union Street. Captain Tennant went in and found the record of the purchase by Ruth Green. The clerk who sold it to her identified Ruth Garrison as "Ruth Green."

The news about Ruth Garrison's confession hit Seattle like a shock wave. People were stunned that a young girl could have planned and executed such a horrible murder. Ruth's friends from Queen Anne high school and the offices where she worked described her as "quiet," "modest," "kind-hearted," "cheerful." Photos of Dudley circulated, and one female columnist expressed her bewilderment that he was so unattractive. Others declared that Ruth must have been hypnotized, that she must be insane.

Friends, family, and a mob of gawkers congregated at the police station to see the girl killer. Soon, flowers and sympathy notes arrived for the perky young teenager. Many insisted that there must be some mistake; that the young girl must surely be innocent. Meanwhile, reports leaked that Ruth herself seemed far more concerned about "Dud's" reaction than about the fact that she had committed murder.

Police filed a charge of first-degree murder against her, and on Thursday morning, two days after the murder, a local alienist, Dr. Donald Nicholson, arrived at the jail to interview her. His report to authorities concluded that Ruth Garrison was not insane.

Meanwhile, Seattle police wanted to talk to Douglas Storrs and they ordered him back to Seattle. When he arrived in town, police took him into custody "for investigation," but did not charge him with any crime.

His story was the same as Ruth's, that Grace had repeatedly threatened to kill herself. He said he never sent for Ruth to come to Okanagan, that she had written to him and then showed up and stayed for four or five days. He admitted that she visited him there twice. He said he did not send Grace any money because he had left her with a large sum. She was living with her father and he figured she had enough. He said he did not bring her with him because they could not find a place to live. He would not say if he loved his wife or Ruth but said he would have brought his wife over if he had been able to find a house. Douglas Storrs issued a statement:

> I never had any agreement with Ruth Garrison that she was to come back here and even talk to my wife. She left there because she had learned what I told her in the first place—that Okanogan was too small a place for us to live and not be found out. She came back here without any plans on my part, except that she would write when she got here and tell me what the situation was.[3]

He claimed that he and Grace had discussed divorce, but he was waiting for her to do it. She was frail and he did not want to shock her by doing it himself. He said the marriage was unhappy and that Grace was unhappy. He was evasive at first when asked about his feelings but soon admitted to reporters that the murder of his wife had not changed his feelings for Ruth, which were "beyond description."

As evidence of Grace's state of mind, he produced an old suicide note, signed by his dead wife. Grace's mother was shown the note and she confirmed it was Grace's handwriting. He also had an affectionate letter that Grace had written to him, discussing her plans to join him soon.

A day later, Sheriff Harry Stark of Okanogan County arrived in Seattle with a warrant that served well to confuse the issue—he charged Storrs with the abduction of Ruth Garrison. A few days later, the sheriff hauled Storrs back to Okanogan.

The commotion at the jailhouse around Ruth's incarceration soon became too much and Sheriff John Stringer arranged "to remove her from morbid surroundings" to a separate facility. He explained that he didn't want to bring her into contact with the sort of women confined in the jail and that "we're humanitarians here." Members of the prosecution objected to the move, saying she was a murderer and "no better than any other woman prisoner."[4]

On April 1, at a hearing packed with a throng of spectators eager to catch a glimpse of Ruth, her defense attorneys, Thomas M. Askren and A. R. Hilen, entered a plea of not guilty by reason of temporary insanity. Her trial was set for May 5. Public interest in the case was so overwhelming city officials hired carpenters to build a fence in the courthouse corridors to manage the crowds.

Before the trial began, Ruth's mother gave an interview to reporters that hinted at Ruth's upcoming defense. She said that when Ruth was sixteen, she had undergone a "catarrhal operation" during which a doctor injected paraffin into her forehead, right between the eyes.

Prominent Seattle physician, Dr. Copeland Plummer, had performed the operation in order to stop Ruth's nose bleeds, though paraffin injections were also used at the time as an early form of cosmetic surgery. The medical community later abandoned the procedure as dangerous, with calamitous results sometimes appearing five to ten years after the injection. Eventual side effects included migration of the paraffin, infection, necrosis, and death. Though Dr. Plummer told reporters the operation had been a success, Mrs. Garrison claimed that Ruth's grades went down afterward and her attitude toward everything changed.

The trial opened on Monday, May 5. Crowds jostled their way into Judge John S. Jurey's courtroom to watch. Numerous spectators noted that Ruth seemed calm and content and even laughed at one point.

The shocker came on Tuesday when defense attorney Asken made his opening statement, blaming Storrs for the death. He declared that "Douglas Storrs was responsible for the murder of his wife, Grace Storrs, when he suggested the crime to Ruth Garrison after he had gotten her into such a weakened condition that she was mentally irresponsible."[5]

The prosecution presented its case quickly with a parade of witnesses, including Grace's mother and sister; the drugstore clerk who sold Ruth the strychnine; William H. Dehn, the chemist who found the strychnine; Captain of Detectives Charles Tennant and Deputy Prosecutor Carmody who obtained Ruth's confession; two nurses at Bon Marché; several waitresses from the tearoom; a reporter who interviewed Ruth after her confession; and the coroner. Alienists Dr. Nicholson and Dr. F. S. Bourns also testified that they had examined Ruth and deemed her to be sane. The defense did not cross-examine any of the prosecution's witnesses, and after less than two hours, the prosecution rested its case.

Askren then rose to begin presenting the defense. He outlined Ruth's impoverished beginnings, the oversized family, and advanced age of her parents. He described how Ruth had left her job by walking out without notifying her employers. She had planned to go to Alaska but wanted to see Douglas one last time. She stayed with him a week in Okanagan, sharing a room with him. During this visit, she began to have fainting spells. Someone told her she was going to be a mother, so Douglas took her to a doctor. Yet she was not pregnant. Askren described how Douglas told the impressionable young Ruth how he wished his wife were out of the picture.

Ruth herself took the stand and testified in her own defense. In a calm, "unfeeling" voice, she described what happened. She said she was wandering around town and had the idea to call Mrs. Storrs and made up her mind to get the strychnine. After Grace began convulsing, she went into the ladies' room and flushed the rest of the small bottle of poison down the toilet.

She told the court she had been out with "Dud" six or seven times before he admitted to her that he was married. The truth only came out when Ruth phoned him at home and Grace answered. Grace learned about the affair when she overheard a conversation between her husband and Ruth, arranging to meet. Grace showed up at the meeting place and confronted her husband and his lover. However, Grace would not leave her husband.

Ruth said, at Douglas's suggestion, she moved out of her aunt and uncle's place and got her own apartment, and she admitted that she had "given in" to Douglas Storrs during her most recent trip to Okanogan.

She talked about the paraffin injections and that she had suffered from a series of hemorrhages. She said she quit school after the operation because her grades "were not satisfactory." Askren pointed out "peculiar red marks on her neck and chest which he said were 'signs of abnormal condition which will be explained later by physicians.'"[6]

Ruth's aunt, Mrs. Clara Rice, testified next. She described a horrific family history, the father's outbursts of temper and how he used to beat Ruth and the other ten children. She said Ruth had always been a nervous child, that she was absent-minded and had "blue spells."

Under cross-examination by prosecutors, she was unable to explain the "nervous" Ruth of her descriptions compared to the serenity of the girl sitting at the defense table. Ruth's mother, Talitha Garrison, took the stand and corroborated the grim family history. At two months old, she declared, little Ruth's father hurled her from her bed. Joseph Garrison, she said, was cruel to all the children and to animals. He was also epileptic, and Ruth had inherited the epilepsy from him.

Ruth's uncle, John Rice, had hosted Ruth for the years when she was in high school. He said she fainted often. Under cross-examination, Carmody got him to admit that Ruth was headstrong, not the weak-willed girl painted by the defense.

A friend of Ruth's from Camano Island testified that Ruth sometimes stopped while walking and began to laugh hysterically. She would stop laughing intermittently and stare at her. Afterward, Ruth seemed to be unaware of what she had been doing.

A defense alienist, Dr. W. G. Williamson of Portland, testified for three hours. He said Ruth suffered from psychopathic epilepsy, with "mental irresponsibilities." He declared that she was mentally irresponsible at the time of the poisoning and had been "psychopathical [sic.] for some years, probably all her life."[7]

He listed a long series of symptoms that demonstrated and contributed to Ruth's insanity: the advanced age of her parents, being the last of eleven children, her father being vicious and a somnambulist, incidents of bed-wetting, a "religious disregard of the truth," and episodes of apparent black-outs, or "blank mind."

He also described physical features, or "personal stigmata," that he regarded as signs of insanity: ears with attached lobules, a high palate, irregular teeth, a nose with widely flaring nostrils, a large upper nasal cavity, breaking out when excited with red splotches upon her chest and neck, cyanosis of the extremities, reflex of the knee and a rapid pupillary reaction of the eyes.

Another defense alienist, Dr. Walter Vose Gulick, said Ruth possessed a "subnormal mentality." He had asked Ruth to name three differences between a king and a president. He insisted that a twelve-year-old should be able to answer it within five to fifteen seconds, but that Ruth took twenty seconds and only gave one answer.

During cross-examination, Carmody asked Gulick to "name three differences between a member of the American house of representatives and a member of the English house of commons."[8] He stared at his wristwatch while twenty seconds passed, and the doctor failed to reply. This earned Carmody a laugh from the crowd of mostly female spectators.

Two more alienists testified about Ruth's below average intelligence, her penchant for "childlike prattle" and lack of remorse—all deemed by them to be symptoms of insanity.

Attorneys presented their closing arguments on May 9. The defense castigated the prosecution for being unkind to young Ruth. To the surprise of many, they did not ask for her freedom but for her to be sent to the insane asylum rather than prison. Though they had opened their case with "temporary insanity," they had reportedly changed their minds about the "temporary" aspect of it after meeting with Ruth's family and hearing the assessment of the defense alienists.

In closing, defense attorney Hilen once again reviewed Ruth's pathetic life. He described her as a baby from a "backwoods cabin" in Virginia. He also trashed Douglas Storrs as a degenerate and blamed him for what happened.

> Just what Ruth saw in Douglas Storrs is beyond our conception. I have never met him, but I have seen his picture, and if I know anything of human nature, it seems to me to suggest degeneracy in every feature.[9]

He claimed that Ruth was in such a weakened mental state that she would do whatever Storrs told her to do, and that Storrs had "made these underhanded suggestions to this child-like mind." He said, "this little epileptic girl is but the instrument by which the real murderer accomplished his purpose."[10]

Prosecuting Attorney Charles E. Claypool flayed the defense, scoffing at the epilepsy defense. He went over the testimony of Dr. Nicholson, who had deemed her sane, and lectured about "the adulterous bed which leads to murder."

The case went to the jury, which deliberated only two hours before returning a verdict: Ruth Garrison was found not guilty due to mental irresponsibility. When she heard the verdict, Ruth smiled, then laughed and kissed her mother. Several jurors cried. As Ruth left the courtroom to be escorted back to her cell, she was laughing gaily.

Within a week, authorities took Ruth by train to the state penitentiary at Walla Walla for treatment of the criminally insane. There was much discussion about transferring her to the asylum at Medical Lake, saying that was a more suitable environment for her, but that institution refused to take her. Walla Walla was ordered to make accommodation. Ruth told reporters she thought it would be nicer at Walla Walla.

A few weeks later, Douglas Storrs went on trial in Okanogan. Officials had withdrawn the puzzling charge of "abduction," and they now charged him with seduction and immorality. Ruth Garrison was slated to be the star witness.

On June 5, guards escorted her out of Walla Walla and to Okanogan. Her attorney, A. R. Hilen, accompanied her. He announced that she had turned against Storrs. On June 6, she took the stand for the prosecution. She again recounted her life story—how she met Storrs and dated him several times before learning he was married. She described several occasions when "Dud" took her to hotels and "made suggestions that I refused to listen to." She described how she had finally submitted to him in Okanogan.

As her testimony continued, and later as the trial wore on, her demeanor changed. She learned how, over the past ten weeks in jail, he had decorated his cell with half a dozen photographs of herself. Her attitude softened toward her former lover. When the defense opened its case, Storrs's attorney, P. D. Smith, recalled her to the stand.

In a stunning moment, Smith made an unexpected announcement to the courtroom and to Ruth: "In the presence of the jurors, Dudley Storrs now offers to marry this girl, and do it now, and I respectfully request that this presiding judge at this trial perform the ceremony here and now."[11]
Ruth's attorney, Hilen, jumped up to object bitterly, saying she was mentally incompetent. He called the offer a "by-play." The prosecutor echoed his anger. "This unfortunate girl, who sits here on the witness stand, may want to marry this defendant, but she shall not."[12]

The discussion degenerated into a shouting match, during which Storrs's attorney argued that the pair loved each other. He also yelled that, "This offer is an absolute bar to further consideration of this case," which may or may not have been the motive behind the marriage proposal.

Hilen insisted that Ruth not be allowed to answer. As a matter of coincidence, the trial judge for Storrs was the same as Ruth's—Judge John S. Jurey. He ruled that "the motion by counsel for the defense that this girl and the defendant be allowed to enter into contract of marriage is denied."[13]

Though she was not allowed to answer her lover's marriage proposal, Ruth henceforth tried during this testimony to offset the damage she had done earlier when testifying for the prosecution. She admitted she loved Dudley. As she left the stand, "Dudley" rewarded her with a big smile.

The prosecution introduced the letters from Grace Storrs to her husband. Another bitter battle arose between attorneys over whether they should be allowed. Judge Jurey ruled that the letters showed that Storrs was still deceiving his wife about his intentions, and that he meant for Grace to join him in Okanogan. He allowed the letters. The prosecution also brought in the hotel proprietor, who testified that Ruth and Douglas had posed as man and wife while staying at his hotel.

After several days, the case went to the jury. They quickly returned their verdict, finding Douglas Storrs guilty of seduction. They sentenced him to the maximum penalty, five years at Walla Walla. The defense announced they would appeal, and defense attorney Smith declared that he himself would raise the $5,000 bail to get his client released.

Ruth requested that she be allowed to see Douglas, but her request was denied. She was upset at the verdict and told anyone who would listen about the great love that existed between herself and "Dud."

Ironically, back at Walla Walla, the two of them occupied cells thirty feet apart. When they learned how close they were, Douglas whistled "Till We Meet Again." She responded by singing, "I Hate to Lose you, 'Cause I'm Used to You Now." Later, she serenaded him with a song called "Daddy" and he whistled another tune called "Oh, Boy."

Storrs's attorney, P. D. Smith, raised his bail money and he was released pending the appeal. He headed to Seattle to stay with his mother. The appeal cited misconduct on the part of Judge John S. Jurey and counsel for the defense, Hilen.

In October 1920, over a year later, the state supreme court upheld the verdict. When the news hit, authorities ordered Douglas back to Walla Walla. In December, he was released again after being granted a re-hearing because the original opinion had been deeply divided.

In April 1921, the court upheld his conviction once again, and Douglas Storrs went back to Walla Walla, where they housed him in a cell house 100 feet away from Ruth, separated by a 15-foot wall.

In November 1922, after Storrs spent about a year and a half at Walla Walla, Acting Governor William Coyle issued a pardon. Coyle said he felt Storrs had been made "the goat." The parole board had recommended the pardon earlier, but Governor Louis F. Hart had refused. By this time, even Judge Jurey was in favor of the pardon. He said he considered Storrs guilty but that he had been punished enough. Reports say that Storrs made no effort to see Ruth, still living at the same prison, before he left.

During the following years, Ruth Garrison and her attorneys made numerous attempts to be granted a sanity hearing. The courts denied all requests until February 1931, after Ruth had spent twelve years in the insanity ward at Walla Walla. This hearing was a success. The state declared that Ruth was sane, and she was released amid much consternation in the press. She was thirty-one years old.

Upon her release, she reportedly went in seclusion and the details of her subsequent life are unknown. One unconfirmed story has her becoming a singer and entertainer known as Jean Ellington who lived in New York City and sang for the radio as "The Girl of the Golden West."

Meanwhile, 1930 census records indicate that Douglas Storrs was living in Los Angeles, married to a woman named Maude. He is shown in 1940 records as still in Los Angeles, but now single. He died in 1967 in Fall City, Washington.

16

A Small Sacrifice (1921)

On a Sunday night in early November 1921, two frightened women made a series of phone calls to Everett police. When officers arrived at the small house on Summit Avenue, they were too late.

Inside the house, they found an agitated mother and her teenaged daughter. Two suitcases sat on the floor, with several freshly laundered sheets resting on top, as though they were about to be packed. Coming from the kitchen, the aroma of stew and corn on the cob. The table was set for three. Stretched out on the floor of the cramped front room was a dead man. He clutched a revolver.

Officers took Bertha Wilkes, thirty-four, and her daughter, Treva, fifteen, downtown, where they signed statements identifying the dead man as Gus Danielson. Bertha and Treva said Gus had shot himself.

August Danielson, age thirty-eight, lived primarily at the Three Lakes Mill, where he worked as a superintendent. He had known Bertha's parents and lately became her suitor. A few years earlier, he had served as executor of the will of Bertha's mother, which included the Summit Avenue cottage and several hundred dollars. Although Gus was a man of means, he spent his weekends at the tiny Wilkes cottage as a "boarder," for which he paid Bertha $15 a week (about $210 in current dollars). He told his attorney that he did so in order to help Bertha pay her bills. He planned to marry Bertha and had already written Treva and Bertha into his will, leaving $4,000 to Bertha (about $57,000) and $1,400 (about $20,000) for Treva's education.

Bertha was a struggling divorcée who had worked at the Sells-Floto circus training baby elephants. She was currently employed as a clerk in a department store and taught dancing for extra money. She had divorced her husband, Emory Pote, and left their young son, Emory Wilson Pote, in the care of relatives in Pennsylvania.

Her history after the divorce is murky. Her daughter, Treva Pote, likely spent time boarding with another family, perhaps while Bertha travelled with the circus. Bertha also reportedly worked the vaudeville circuit. Her maiden name was Thompson, so the origin of the name "Wilkes" is a mystery. It may have been a stage name or there might have been another brief marriage after her divorce from Pote. These were all facts that would work against her in the coming months.

Although the women originally told police that Gus had killed himself, it did not take the coroner long to establish that he had been shot three times— once in the forearm, once in the neck, and once in the back. Bertha's lawyer, Samuel A. Bostwick, quickly explained that Gus had been drinking and had started an argument that ended up in a scuffle. The gun had gone off when it dropped during the fight.

Three days after the shooting, on Wednesday, November 9, police arrested Bertha Wilkes for the murder of Gus Danielson. Prosecuting Attorney Thomas A. Stiger pointed out, perhaps unnecessarily, that Gus could not possibly have shot himself several times, including once in the back. He declared that Bertha had shot him while he was packing up his suitcase to leave the house after a quarrel. He listed several motives, all financial: the money he left to her and Treva in his will, a generous life insurance payout, and a considerable amount of property he owned back in Sweden. The charge was murder in the first degree.

Police also arrested fifteen-year-old Treva Pote and took her to the juvenile detention center. Apparently, they initially charged her with murder as well but eventually changed it to accessory. After a delay caused by defense attorney Bostwick's illness, the court tried mother and daughter together in late January 1922. Bertha was said to be near collapse and not coping well, while Treva was "light-hearted as a lark."[1]

The trial opened to a packed courtroom. Having two women on trial for murder caused a massive sensation. The fact that both of them were attractive heightened public interest. Treva, especially, drew praise from reporters, who invariably described her as a "dainty little thing." She dressed like a flapper, which attracted the support of those who flouted society's conventions. The case also became a cause célèbre for women as details filtered out about Danielson being a bully.

The court had difficulty seating a jury because the prosecution was asking for the death penalty. If the state were successful, Bertha Wilkes and Treva Pote would be executed by hanging. This was not an image that appealed to many potential jurors, and the prosecution rejected anyone who said they would have a problem with that.

The defense also objected to numerous potential jurors. They ruled out anyone who adhered to strict social norms, asking if they had anything against people who went to the movies on Sunday instead of to church.

They also asked how they felt about Prohibition, which had become U.S. law in 1919 and in Washington State in 1914. The defense rejected those who disapproved of vaudeville, the circus, or of having "a little cider" in the house.

When the trial finally started, officials escorted Bertha and Treva into the courtroom. Bertha came in, "her eyes blood-shot, pale, leaning on her daughter's arm." Treva reportedly looked undaunted by what was happening. One reporter gushed about her rosy cheeks and shining eyes:

> [H]er slender figure daintily gowned, she seemed a thing entirely apart from the grim tragedy which has thrown a sinister shadow across her life. Her eyes were warm with love and sorrow as she sat, clasping her mother's hand.[2]

The prosecution's opening statement outlined "what sort of woman" Bertha was, including the fact of her divorce and how she left her husband to go off with the Sells-Floto circus. He described a scene where Bertha shot Gus in the back while he packed and went into detail about the amount of money she hoped to gain from his death.

Defense attorney Samuel Bostwick was a man of surplus personality, and he made the most of the dramatic trial. He constantly referred to Treva as "a cute little thing," remarking more than once about the great crowd that had gathered to see the spectacle. Before the trial began, he had warned reporters that he would be making an opening statement that would cause a tremendous stir, and he did not disappoint.

When his turn came to speak, he came immediately to the point. He announced that the cute little thing, Treva Pote, would testify that she had, in fact, fired the shots that killed Gus Danielson. He said he would prove that "Danielson was a fiend, a man of ungovernable temper, who had attacked both Mrs. Wilkes and her daughter before, and of whom they stood in mortal dread."[3]

He said that on the night of the shooting, Gus had marched over to a neighbor's home, where Bertha had been visiting. He made a scene there, cursing Bertha because his dinner was not ready. Bertha went home with him but objected to this treatment, at which a great argument erupted. Gus physically attacked Bertha, pinning her on the couch and strangling her. Just as she was passing out, she heard two shots. The next thing she knew, Gus had let go of her throat and was lying on the floor. "Treva will go on the stand and tell you how those shots were fired," Bostwick said.[4] During this speech to the stunned courtroom, both Treva and Bertha were crying.

A great deal of legal wrangling followed Bostwick's opening statement, during which he tried to get the judge to dismiss the charges against the two women. In a mystifying about-face, Judge Guy C. Alston at first dismissed the charges against Treva, then angrily changed his mind when Bostwick tried to get the same for Bertha. In a fit of pique, Judge Alston vacated the ruling about Treva that he had made minutes earlier, and the trial continued as before.

The prosecution's case consisted primarily of testimony from the police officers who worked the crime scene. One officer reiterated how Gus could not have shot himself as the women initially said, though he pointed out that Bertha's neck and arms looked heavily bruised.

Gus's lawyer, Daniel Locke, provided a motive for the shooting, confirming that Bertha did indeed know that she and Treva were featured prominently in Gus's will. He said that Bertha had spoken at length before the shooting about how she would like to see Treva get a good education with the money.

On February 1, Bertha Wilkes took the stand in her own defense. She said that Gus had previously threatened to "knock my dam' block off," and described her version of the events that took place that evening. She testified:

> I was over at Mrs. Stockweather's house about 5:30 that evening … when Gus called me up and asked "Why aren't you home? Get home, where you belong." I told him that I'd be right over. At the next moment the back door came bustin' open and Gus came in in his shirt sleeves.
>
> "Well, are you coming?" he asked.
>
> "Yes," I told him.
>
> "G—d--- it, then come on," he said.
>
> "How do you get that way?" I asked him. Then he beat it.
>
> When I got in my kitchen, he was waiting for me. And I told him, "Say Gus, what's the matter with you? How do you get this way? My land, don't you know it looks bad for you to be bossing me this way in front of folks?"
>
> "Well, why the h--- ain't you home," he replied.
>
> "Say," I told him. 'I ain't wearing no ring. I ain't married to you. You can't boss me."
>
> "I'll show you," he said. "I don't give a d--- what people think. You ought to be home where you belong."[5]

Bertha went on to describe how Gus then demanded his supper, at which she retorted that he could serve himself. He marched into the front room, at which point she thought he was packing his things to go. Instead, he called her into the room, saying he had something else to say to her. She told him to go away. He responded by saying, "I want to tell you I'm going to kill you." She threatened to call the police, which is when he swore at her and hit her. She got away from him and called the police.

> When I got back from the phone he had his gun. He was awful. I knew he was going to kill me, and I grabbed him quick. He pushed me back on

the couch. I fell over and almost lost my hold, as I wrestled with him. He choked me—I got his hands again—I heard a shot.[6]

She said she remembered hearing the gun fall and she yelled at Treva to grab it.

He was just snorting and blowing, he was so wild—his eyes stuck out of his head—there was a pause. Then there was some more shots and—and I saw him lying there. I was afraid to look. I was so afraid my daughter was shot.[7]

She asked Gus what happened, but he did not answer. She asked Treva what happened, and she did not answer either. She phoned the police again, then went and shook Gus but he did not respond. Finally, the police arrived and declared that Gus was dead.

Another witness took the stand and confirmed Gus Danielson's bad temper. Charles Coonan, a "bent and gnarled," gnome-like fellow with a "huge beard" worked at the Three Lakes Mill as a night watchman. He caused a stir in the courtroom with his vivid testimony. "When Gus Danielson got mad," he declared, waving his arms excitedly, "my golly! He got mad all over. It's an awful thing, I tell you, for him to get mad."[8]

The kooky atmosphere in the courtroom went even more afield with the next witness, Treva Pote—not necessarily because of her testimony but because of the repeated interventions of Judge Alston. As soon as Treva took the stand, Alston sent the jury out of the room. He asked Treva how old she was.

"Fifteen, sir," she replied. Although her childish treble was faint, it penetrated to the farthest corner of the court room, so tense was the moment.

"Don't you admit that you shot that man if you didn't," Judge Alston told her, in a voice that trembled with emotion. "If you did it, say so, but you've got your life to live, and if you didn't shoot him, for God's sake don't say you did."

The girl nodded, a look half of terror, half of gratitude in her big brightened eyes.[9]

The jury came back in and Treva began her testimony, describing what happened that night. She said she had phoned the police while her mother and Gus quarreled. Gus pulled a gun and Bertha struggled with him for it. Gus pushed Bertha onto the couch and was choking her when the gun "exploded." It fell and her mother kicked it and yelled at her to get it. She picked it up, and she squeezed the trigger twice before throwing the pistol away. She described Gus in the same terms that her mother had used ("his eyes bulging out of his head"). The prosecution asked her to pick up the revolver and show the court how she held the gun as she fired. She refused and as he pressed her, she began to cry. Finally, Bertha burst out:

"Oh, if I had known—if I had only known," she shrieked. "I'd never have let her take the stand! Why didn't you tell me that you shot him, Treva! Why didn't you tell me." And this to Bostwick—"My little girl is innocent."

"You bet she's innocent," Judge Alston interposed.[10]

Judge Alston once again ordered the jury out. When they were gone, he turned to Treva and delivered a stunning lecture. He accused her of lying and lectured her that she should not sacrifice herself for her mother. He asked her why she had not broken down like this on the night of the shooting.

At this point, Bertha went "into hysterics." Alston told her to keep quiet. "This girl is just as innocent as I am; and you—" pointing his finger at Defense Attorney S. A. Bostwick "—and you have made her testify to this."[11] The defense objected but Alston continued:

> The real tragedy was not pulled off at 1612 Summit Ave. It is being enacted here in this courtroom. That innocent little girl is being forced to testify to a lie. That little girl never had the gun in her hands.[12]

Despite Judge Alston's efforts, Treva refused to change her testimony. After nearly a week, the defense and prosecution both rested. The next morning, when court resumed for closing arguments, Prosecuting Attorney Stiger made a dramatic announcement:

> "Evidence has come to me since the state and defense rested that Treva Pote has made the statement since the closing of the case by us that she did not touch the revolver or discharge it and also has made the statement that the shooting was by the mother. I ask the court to reopen the case that the truth may be known."
>
> The judge responded: "No one can doubt that that little girl is now being made a living sacrifice," declared Judge Alston. "To whom was the statement made?"
>
> "I have the gentleman inside the courtroom," answered the prosecutor.
>
> "Where is the man?" queried the judge. "Bring him in."
>
> A young man stepped forward from the front of the courtroom into which he had been ushered not ten minutes before.
>
> "Treva, do you know this young man?" was the solemn question of the judge.[13]

The crowded courtroom was silent, waiting for Treva's answer. Finally, she mumbled, "no," then said faintly, "I don't know." Her mother's head dropped, and she covered her face with her hands.

"Who is that man?" asked the judge.

The young man said he was Fred Murray and in answer to the judge's question he said he had talked with Treva the night before at the detention home where she stays and that she had said she had not discharged the revolver.

"Stool pigeon," roared the defense attorney.

"Aw, what's the matter with you?" growled the prosecutor.

"That girl is as innocent of this crime as the court reporter. I will take a few minutes recess and look up references on reopening the case," announced the judge.[14]

When the judge returned, he announced he could find no precedent for the situation. The state asked him to proceed without a precedent. The judge, musing aloud, complained again about Bertha. "This mother, who has dragged this little girl in to defend her, dragged her in as a vicarious sacrifice. No one who has watched these episodes has doubted this."[15]

Finally, Judge Alston addressed Treva again, asking her if she wanted to get this off her conscience. She did not answer. He prompted her again and she said, "I have nothing to get off my conscience."

With that, Judge Alston ruled that he would not reopen the case. The closing statements moved forward and the case went to the jury that afternoon at 4:36 p.m. At 6 p.m. the jury went out for dinner. By 7:15 p.m., they had returned and taken the first ballot. The verdict was unanimous: acquittal for Treva and acquittal for Bertha.

> Cheers and handclapping echoed through the courtroom as the verdict was read to the audience of almost 200. Members of the jury sought out the defendants to congratulate them. The mother was calm and self-possessed, the girl cheerful and composed.[16]

Friends of Bertha and Treva, Mr. and Mrs. Earl Monohan, whisked them away. The Monohans had also testified as to Bertha's good character. A couple days later, Bertha suffered a collapse and required the care of doctors. She later told curious reporters that she might leave town to get away from those who disapproved of her. She suggested she might put Treva into a boarding school, paid for by the bequest from Gus Danielson, and join the circus again.

Rumors circulated that Gus may have had one or more illegitimate offspring back in Sweden who would try to break his will, but most agreed that Bertha and Treva would not be hindered in collecting their inheritance.

A year later, Treva apparently decided against her mother's plans for an education. On March 16, 1923, at age sixteen, she married thirty-two-year-old Edward Charles Zempel, a divorced credit manager.

17

The Trunk Murder (1921)

When a thirty-eight-year-old ex-con married a sixty-eight-year-old divorcée with a tidy pile of money, it was no surprise that trouble popped up.

Kate Moores may not have known about James Mahoney's conviction for drugging and robbing a man in Spokane back in 1918. When she met him, he was freshly paroled from his six to eight-year sentence in the state penitentiary. He had served only three years when his attorney—an old family friend who was tight with the governor—got him released.

Kate was a tough woman; she told one friend that no man would ever get hold of her money or property. She enjoyed showing off her jewelry and was also known to dance a jig. She wore wigs due to hair loss, and specialized dentures, since she had only a few teeth left. Reportedly born Kate Algier in 1853, the daughter of a roadhouse operator from Butte, Montana, the rumor was she had once been a dance hall girl back in the wild frontier days of that state.

Her past may have featured more than one discarded or deceased husband, but the spouse who counted was Dr. Charles Moores, an optometrist, known then as an "oculist." Though the marriage did not work out, it proved beneficial to Kate. After their divorce, she owned the New Baker hotel at 2327 First Avenue, the Sofia apartments at 409 Denny Way, a rental property at 2720 Fourth Avenue, plus $25,000 worth of jewelry (worth over $350 thousand in current money). Overall, Kate Moores was worth over $200,000 ($2.5 million in today's money).

James Mahoney's mother, Nora Mahoney, worked for Kate as a manager of the Sofia apartments. When her darling boy, James, got sprung from Walla Walla, he came home to his mom and sister in December 1920. In less than two months, on February 10, 1921, James Mahoney married his mother's boss. Kate told a friend that James was a "good boy" who treated her right.

In mid-April, friends saw Kate around town, preparing for a honeymoon to St. Paul, Minnesota, with her fresh young husband. Despite Kate's considerable wealth, she and James lived at the Sofia apartments, the same building where Nora and her daughter, Dolly, lived. An unknown number of other tenants also resided in the apartment building, and some of them had to walk through Kate's kitchen in order to get to the shared bathroom. These tenants were among the last people to see Kate alive, on the night of April 16, 1921.

A tenant had walked through the Mahoney's kitchen in order to prepare a bath for her husband. She overheard Kate and James cooking together, and Kate was explaining to her husband the best way to choose a potato at the market. Later that evening, the Mahoney family was listening to music, and Kate was dancing an Irish jig with James's twelve-year-old niece.

Kate and James Mahoney reportedly left the next day for their honeymoon in St. Paul. Everything seemed normal until, late in April, James Mahoney returned alone. He told others that he and Kate had met a friendly couple on the train, and that Kate had decided to continue traveling with the couple, first to New York City and then on to Havana, Cuba.

James also had a set of documents with him, signed by his wife. One document was a power of attorney giving James control over Kate's properties and bank accounts. Furthermore, the company who managed her rental property at 2720 Fourth Avenue received a typewritten letter from Kate, giving James the right to collect the rents.

Kate had two nieces, both of whom had long been her heirs if she were to die. When they learned James had returned without Kate, they became concerned. They considered his behavior suspicious and they thought it strange they had not heard from their aunt. On May 3, they took their story to police. The nieces, Mrs. Kate Stewart and Mrs. Carrie Hewitt, told police about their elderly aunt's quickie marriage to James Mahoney and insisted that the signed documents Mahoney was showing around were forged.

Police were very interested. It is likely they quickly discovered that he was an ex-con out on parole, a fact that normally would have kept him confined to Washington State. However, it turned out the authorities had given him very favorable terms on his parole, which allowed him to travel out of state— probably the work of his well-connected lawyer.

Lee Johnston, Mahoney's lawyer, said that James had come to his office after his return from Minnesota and said he had a postcard from Kate in Havana. It was apparent that Mahoney never actually produced the postcard. Johnston also claimed that he knew Kate and that her signature on the power of attorney was genuine.

Nevertheless, police arrested Mahoney, charging him with forgery. When they brought him in, they discovered a diamond necklace in his coat pocket, valued at $10,000 ($143,000 in today's money). Failing to locate Kate, investigators opened a murder inquiry. By the end of May, newspapers reported that police were dragging Lake Union for a trunk.

It turned out that on the night of April 16, the night before Kate and James had supposedly left for their honeymoon, James had called an express service to come and pick up a large trunk. The delivery man came at about 9 o'clock. When he arrived, James led him up the stairs to a hallway where the trunk sat. The two men carried it downstairs and put it in the truck. They drove to Lake Union, near Howard and Son's canoe factory. They loaded the trunk into a small white rowboat. James then climbed into the boat and disappeared out onto the dark lake. The delivery man told police he believed at the time that the trunk was probably full of whiskey, which was against the law.

Police held James on $10,000 bail, which was a very high amount. Witnesses came forward with claims about having seen him out in the boat that night. The boat rental company said he had rented the boat for a week and that he had never returned it. Searchers later found it submerged near the shore.

E. J. Brandt, a notary, told police that a woman had come to his office, identifying herself as Kate Mahoney. She asked him to notarize the power of attorney document granting rights to James Mahoney. It turned out that Brandt knew Kate Moores but did not know that she had married Mahoney. He only made the connection when he read in the paper that Kate was missing, and he realized that Kate Mahoney was the woman he knew as Kate Moores. He said the woman who came to his office was not Kate Moores.

On August 8, 1921, police were still dragging Lake Union, looking for the missing trunk. In Portage Bay, their equipment hit something, but they were unable to identify what it was. Later the same day in the same area, a tug called the *Audrey* came upon a trunk floating upside-down in the water. There was evidence that the trunk had been tied to something with ropes and that something had severed the ropes. They notified authorities.

When police opened the trunk, they found at the top a blue plush coat with three buttons torn away. Beneath that was a small blood-stained rug, a bloody mandarin coat, then a pink and white striped house dress, a blue bath robe and some women's underclothing. Underneath it all, they found the nude body of a woman with towels wrapped around her head. Beneath the towels, the head had been covered with lime. The features were unrecognizable. There was a large hole in the skull's temple and another dent on the back of the skull. Other abrasions were obvious. The woman had been dead for about three months.

They found a plain gold wedding band on the ring finger of the left hand. There were no teeth in the upper jaw and only three in the lower. They found a "gilmore attachment" anchored to the remaining teeth. This was the device that allowed Kate's dentist, Dr. Wood, to identify her. He declared that he had done the work himself.

Later, authorities announced that Kate had first been knocked out with an enormous amount of morphine. Police surmised that after drugging her, James had stuffed her into the trunk. Since they could find no trace of blood in the apartment, they believed he had probably used a hammer to bash in her skull when she was already in the trunk.

On Wednesday, August 10, police charged James Mahoney with first degree murder. His attorney said he would plead not guilty. The case was a huge sensation, generating numerous headlines. Crowds of people flocked to the morgue to view the body.

Meanwhile, James Mahoney suddenly went insane in his cell. Newspaper reports describe him playing peek-a-boo with his jailers and complaining that his clothes were full of pins and needles. He failed to recognize his mother and sister. Based on his strange behavior, Lee Johnston, his attorney, filed an insanity complaint. He said Mahoney would not even talk to him to discuss his defense.

The court appointed a medical commission to examine Mahoney and determine his fitness for trial. They concluded that he was perfectly sane and quite able to distinguish right from wrong.

By mid-August, when Mahoney was bleating like a sheep in his cell, nobody paid much attention. When he went to court to enter his plea, he still refused to speak. The default plea was "not guilty." His murder trial was scheduled for September 20. When the coroner's report came out, it said that Kate had between ten and fifteen grains of morphine in her, enough to kill fifteen people.

When the trial began on September 20, the enormous headline on the front page of the *Seattle Star* was "MAHONEY YAWNS AT TRIAL!" The day before, he had given an interview to the paper, during which he had acted crazy and rambled on about going to Mexico. Lee Johnston tried to abort the trial for jurisdiction reasons, then demanded a change of venue. The judge said "no."

The prosecution laid out their case in their opening statement. They described how, in the days before her disappearance, Kate had gone around town getting ready for her honeymoon trip. At the same time, her husband was making arrangements to commit murder.

They described how, on Friday, April 15, Kate had gone to her safe deposit box and bought travelers' checks for $460. She told several people she was leaving on Sunday for her honeymoon. Neighbors had last seen her on Saturday evening.

The previous Wednesday, April 13, James had rented half of a double houseboat on Lake Union. He told the owners that he planned to spend the summer in the houseboat with a partner. On Friday, April 15, he went again to the lake and rented the rowboat, paying for a week. He gave the name

Glassford. On Saturday, April 16, James went to a hardware store and bought 30 feet of rope and 5 lb of lime.

On Sunday, April 17, James went to Everett and took a Great Northern train to St. Paul. He registered at a hotel there as James E. Mahoney and wife. He wrote letters to Kate's relatives, forging her name. He cashed some traveler's checks. He returned to Seattle in late April and filed a forged document giving him power of attorney over Kate's property. He drove around town in Kate's sedan and made several efforts to convert her property into cash. He collected rents. He told everyone that his wife was enjoying her vacation in Havana.

The prosecution's case against him was circumstantial because they had found no blood or other evidence of an actual murder in the apartment. One of several star witnesses was Alvin Jorgenson, the delivery man who had hauled the trunk to Lake Union. On the stand, he described again the process of hauling the trunk out to the lake with James and gave a detailed description of the trunk itself. Defense attorney Lee Johnston went after Jorgenson's testimony, questioning how he could describe that particular trunk but no others that he handled that night. He insisted that Jorgenson describe other trunks he had handled, but Jorgenson could not. He also pressed him on his identification of James and Jorgenson admitted he had refreshed his memory from the office records. During their rebuttal, the prosecutor asked Jorgenson how often he had hauled a round-top trunk at night to a dark place, and he answered, "Once in four years."

Another witness testified that Kate withdrew $1,600 from her safe deposit box and told him that they were leaving the next day. She said James was going to "sell a patent and get a lot of money." She said she did not put all her cash into travelers' checks because "Jim didn't want me to," due to the trouble of cashing them.

Other important witnesses were a pair of brothers who had known James in the past. One brother testified he saw him in mid-April and that James told him he was going east that night. The other brother took James to the train station. James had said nothing about being married, and there was no sign of a wife. One brother got a letter from James in St. Paul, dated April 23. The letter did not mention a wife or a honeymoon.

While Kate's dentures were passed around among the jurors, her dentist testified that he recognized the unique bridge work from the body in the trunk. He said Kate's mouth was "peculiar," and that he had created the bridge system himself and it was not something taught in college. Johnston pressed him on how he could be so sure. The dentist compared mouths with the uniqueness of fingerprints, saying that no two were alike.

Johnston tried to get discussions of the forged documents omitted because the forgery charges against James were a separate case. The judge overruled him. The state brought in Mrs. Myra E. Helm, a stenographer and bookkeeper who worked at a hotel in St. Paul where "J. E. Mahoney and wife" had registered on April 22. James had asked her to do some typewriting for him. He dictated two letters, both purporting to be from Mrs. J. E. Mahoney. One was to Kate's Seattle lawyer and another was for her Seattle banker. The lawyer's letter asked him to turn over to James "all abstracts and so forth now in your possession." The banker's letter authorized James to use her safe deposit box, "the key to which he has in his possession."

Kate's niece, Carrie E. Hewett, came to the stand and identified her Aunt Kate's jewelry, the pieces found on Mahoney's person. At several points during the trial, the battle between Lee Johnston and prosecutor Malcom Douglas grew so heated, some spectators claimed they almost came to blows. The circus-like atmosphere was fed by the fact that James's young niece, twelve-year-old Margaret, sat next to her uncle during the entire trial, snuggling with him, whispering and laughing.

Despite James's "crazy" antics, defense attorney Johnston did not go for the insanity defense. Instead, he used a multi-pronged strategy. He claimed that the body in the trunk was not Kate Mahoney and that the police had planted the trunk in the lake. He said that James had an alibi in the form of a Mrs. Atkinson and her son, D. I. Atkinson. The Atkinsons reportedly met James and Kate on the train and were the friendly people with whom Kate had traveled to Cuba.

Mysteriously, newspapers reported that D. I. Atkinson was in Seattle, but for reasons not explained by anyone, police had arrested him. Neither of the Atkinsons appeared at the trial.

Johnston worked hard to throw doubt on the timeline of events on the weekend in question. Witnesses testified that they had seen Kate later than the time indicated by Jorgenson, the transport man. One neighbor insisted she had seen the trunk in the hallway that night but that she had seen it again several days later in the Mahoney living room.

Mahoney's sister, Dolores "Dolly" Johnson testified that she had talked to Kate two hours after Mahoney supposedly stuffed Kate into the trunk. She said Kate and young Margaret were dancing to Irish tunes up to about 11 p.m.; she also claimed that she talked to Kate on the phone on Sunday, April 17.

James Mahoney's niece, Margaret, also testified that she had talked to "Aunt Katie" on Sunday on the phone. The family all testified they had been dancing Irish jigs until 11 p.m. with other friends, including a man named Gus Johnson. However, Gus Johnson later broke this alibi when he said he was not even there that Saturday night.

The defense found a dentist to come to the stand and dispute the testimony of Kate's dentist. Johnston also called an attendant at the bank who said the signature on the power of attorney document was indeed Kate Mahoney's. A man said he had seen Kate on May 31 or June 1 in Seattle. Others said they had seen her after she was supposedly dead.

During the testimony of a police detective, Johnston grilled him about the condition of two different ropes that had been found on the trunk. One rope was covered with sea growth, but the other was clean. This, Johnston yelled, proved that the trunk had been planted by police. Meanwhile, it came out that Johnston's legal firm was being paid with Kate's money—that in payment for their services, James Mahoney had given them deeds to her property.

In his closing arguments, Johnston insisted that Mahoney had been framed and that "hypnotic influence" had been used upon Alvin Jorgenson, the transport man. After about ten days, the case went to the jury. They deliberated only four hours before returning their verdict: James Mahoney was guilty of first-degree murder. They gave him the death penalty. Lee Johnston filed an appeal. James went back to jail, where he complained to reporters that he wanted to write down his life story but that his jailers refused to give him a writing table.

A couple days later, police issued a warrant for Dorothy Johnson, Mahoney's sister, on the charges of grand larceny and forgery. Prosecutors said she helped prepare the forged power of attorney, and that she was the woman posing as Kate Mahoney in the offices of the notary, Brandt. The grand larceny charges were unrelated to the murder case.

Dorothy went on trial in late November. Although Brandt could not positively identify her as the "fake Kate," a janitor from the building ID'd her as the woman he directed to the notary's office. Prosecutors also argued that Dorothy must have known about the murder, and that she certainly knew that Kate was dead. Shortly after April 16, she had told Margaret to go down and have the phone listing changed from Kate's name. Although the defense tried to get her off by saying she was pregnant, a jury found Dorothy guilty of forgery. She was sentenced to five to twenty years. In early 1923, before going off to prison, Dorothy tried to save the life of her brother by making a false confession to the murder of Kate Mahoney.

James Mahoney's appeal failed, and officials set his execution date set for December 1, 1922. Initially, he did not want to talk to a priest, but his niece Margaret reportedly convinced him to seek salvation with Father Stephen Buckley. Father Buckley stayed with him through his final night. Early on December 1, prison officials escorted James Mahoney to the scaffold, where the executioner placed a noose around his neck. He made no final statement. At 7:02 a.m., the trap was sprung, and, at 7:08 a.m., the prison physician pronounced him dead.

It later emerged that, shortly after their marriage, James and Kate Mahoney had gone together to an attorney and drawn up wills that left their property to each other. Yet a few days later, Kate Mahoney returned alone and had her lawyer draw up a new, superseding will, leaving all her money and property to her two nieces, Carrie Hewitt and Kate Stewart.

18

The Case of the Comely Killer (1921)

On a Monday in early August 1918, twenty-four-year-old Clara Skarin lay in a Seattle hospital bed with a gunshot wound in her leg. She told police she had been shot in her own home at 15 Harrison Street by a woman named Cleo Winborn. Cleo had also shot Clara's mother, Emma Skarin, who lived in the same home. Emma died immediately. Cleo, who had worked as a pianist in the theater and had once played the piano for her local church in Montana, then shot and killed herself. Clara was the only person at the scene who survived. At Clara's hospital bedside was Cleo's fifty-year-old husband, Robert L. Winborn, a Seattle barber.

Newspapers printed conflicting details about what happened. Clara reportedly told police that Cleo Winborn was "insanely jealous" over her friendship with Robert, even though he had never been unfaithful with Clara and all they did was lunch together and walk home together.

In one version of the story, Cleo showed up at Clara's home brandishing the loaded revolver and confronted Clara. Cleo was shouting at her and Clara turned to walk away. In a window's reflection, Clara saw Cleo raising her arm. She quickly turned and struck Cleo's arm as the gun went off. She felt something in her hip and the two women grappled over the gun. Emma Skarin ran into the room. Another shot rang out and Clara fainted. When Clara came to, both of the other women were dead.

Another story had Cleo arguing with Emma. When Clara entered the room, Cleo fired at her, but Emma jumped in the way and took the bullet for her daughter. Like many episodes in the life of Clara Skarin, the actual facts lay hidden somewhere among a pile of murky details that might or might not be true.

Clara's father, Philip Skarin, had died in 1907 when Clara was thirteen years old. Emma Skarin took a job as a housekeeper for a wealthy German immigrant who had made a fortune in Seattle real estate. Ferdinand Hochbrunn, a lifetime bachelor, was an aggressive businessman and several people had sued him over deals that had gone sour. However, he took in the mother and daughter and reportedly paid for Clara's schooling.

By the time Clara was sixteen, in 1910, she already worked full-time as a stenographer. She and Emma lived with Ferdinand at 2520 Fifth Avenue in Seattle. When she was twenty-two, Clara moved into the apartment at 15 Harrison Street; Emma came with her. Two years later, in 1918, Cleo Winborn burst into their apartment with her revolver.

Shortly after Clara got out of the hospital, Robert Winborn returned to his former home in Detroit. At some point, Clara followed him to Michigan. In the summer of 1919, about a year after the shooting, Robert was sick and dying in a hospital at Kalamazoo. This time, Clara sat at his bedside. On September 4, 1919, he died at age fifty-one. His death certificate said he died of epilepsy.

It appears that Clara may have married him on his deathbed, although she later denied it. His death certificate listed him as married, not widowed, and that the informant of his death was "Mrs. Robert L. Winborn." She remained in Kalamazoo, working as a stenographer under the name of Clara Winborn, identifying herself as a widow.

At some point, she contacted her old benefactor, Ferdinand Hochbrunn, and he sent her money and a ticket back to Seattle; this set the stage for the next violent episode in Clara's young life.

In late December 1921, plumbers were called to the apartment building at 2520 Fifth Avenue, Seattle. The downstairs residents, who were Ferdinand's tenants, had reported water leaking through the ceiling from a burst pipe in Ferdinand's apartment. He had been out of town since October.

The tenant, Pierre Chedotal, went into the upstairs apartment with the plumber. Inside, they discovered the body of seventy-two-year-old Ferdinand Hochbrunn sprawled on the floor and partly covered with a blanket.

Pierre and his wife, Jeanne, called the police. They told detectives they had last seen Ferdinand on October 19, more than two months earlier. On that date, Ferdinand's "ward," Clara Skarin, had visited the apartment and they saw her leave. Later, they overheard Ferdinand arguing with a man. Since then, on several occasions, they had heard him shuffling around.

Clara, they said, had lived with Ferdinand for several months over the summer and fall. He told them she was the daughter of a former housekeeper, and that she had "suffered a sunstroke in Chicago, was in poor health and had come at his request, to live with him as a daughter, to recuperate and attend to household duties."[1] Sometime in early October, she had moved in with her aunt in Seattle.

Several times during November, they had spotted Clara using her key to get into the apartment. Clara told them that Ferdinand had gone to Portland. She said he had asked her to look after the apartment and pay the bills for him. However, they had not seen her since the last Sunday in November, nearly a month before they found Ferdinand's body. Police became concerned over Clara's whereabouts and worried she might also have been murdered or perhaps kidnapped. There was also confusion about her name—some called her Clara Skarin and others said she was Mrs. Betty Winborn.

Ferdinand Hochbrunn had been shot. The coroner removed a 0.32 caliber bullet from his skull and indicated that he had been dead for some time. Someone had slit open the pockets of his trousers. Police assumed that the killer did not want to insert their hand into the dead man's pockets to steal the contents because they were superstitious. Police assumed the motive for the murder was robbery.

Investigators located Clara's aunt, who told them that Clara had left town. The mystery deepened when investigators interviewed Ferdinand's attorney, Edward von Tobel, a well-known Seattle pioneer.

Von Tobel was very much surprised to learn that his client had been dead for some time, since he had been corresponding with him regularly. In fact, in response to telegraphed and written instructions from Ferdinand, von Tobel had been forwarding rental income to his client at various hotels in Portland, San Francisco, and San Bernardino. Seattle police notified officials in those cities to check out the hotels indicated by von Tobel and apprehend whomever was impersonating the dead man.

Meanwhile, stories surfaced about Ferdinand's real estate lawsuits and enemies. Several years earlier, he had been attacked, beaten, and left unconscious. Police had never identified his assailant. Some said that Hochbrunn knew who it was but for some reason did not pursue charges.

While searching his apartment, police discovered $2,000 in currency locked in a trunk. They found his will, which bequeathed all of his considerable holdings to his brother in San Francisco and a sister in Germany.

Police also found another trunk in what the neighbors said was Clara's room. Inside, they discovered old letters and telegrams from Robert Winborn addressed to Clara E. Skarin; other letters were addressed to Clara Winborn.

Neighbors said that while Clara was living there, they had seen her meeting furtively with an unknown man. They described Clara heading up the street by herself. The man would appear and fall in behind her and they would talk. Only after they were away from the apartment building would they actually walk together. The man never came to the house.

Meanwhile, Clara's distraught aunt and uncle, Mrs. and Mrs. W. G. Datesman, stopped cooperating with police. They were angry about suggestions that their beloved niece might be involved in shooting Ferdinand. They said Clara had eaten Thanksgiving dinner at their home and left for Santa Barbara due to ill health. The story generated sensational headlines and reporters had been camped outside of their home until Mr. Datesman swore at them and sent them away.

The attorney, von Tobel, also defended Clara. If she was involved, he insisted, there must be an accomplice directing her. Wild theories circulated around Seattle: Clara discovered Ferdinand's body, immediately went insane and either fled or killed herself; Clara fell into the clutches of a mystery murderer who killed both Ferdinand and her.

Clara's cousin, Mrs. Anna Clark, said that she and her toddler had accompanied Clara into the apartment in mid-November. Clara told her that Ferdinand was in California and that she had to pay the bills for light and water. Anna did not see a body, though she admitted she did not go into that room.

One reporter, Hal Armstrong at the *Seattle Star*, wrote long columns musing about what poor Clara must have felt as she poked around in the apartment fetching her clothes, carefully avoiding the horrifying body under the blanket. Armstrong staged a contest in the pages of the *Star*, asking amateur detectives to solve the mystery and send their solutions to him. The *Star* also printed poems that Clara had clipped from magazines, which police had found in her trunk.

Witnesses reported sightings of Clara. Someone saw her in Portland in late November, using the name Betty Winborn. Another saw her in Santa Barbara the day after Christmas. A handwriting expert examined the communications von Tobel had received. He confirmed they were forgeries. He also compared Clara's handwriting and concluded that Clara was the forger.

Another investigator reported that Ferdinand had stored a hoard of gold coins in a large tin box that he kept in his trunk. Police had found the tin box, but it was empty. The Chedotals claimed they had seen Clara with the tin box and had also seen her paying Ferdinand's bills with gold coins.

The new year came and went with no sign of Clara. A month passed, then another. By March, reporters had moved on to other stories, police had moved on to other cases. They abandoned the search for Clara Skarin/ Betty Winborn.

Nearly a year later, in early September 1922, a couple of Seattle residents were visiting Oakland, California. They had cause to go into the offices of the electric company in that city, and there they spotted a stenographer named Betty Parrish working in the office. The Seattleites quickly notified police that they had found Clara Skarin.

Local police arrested Clara, and lieutenant of detectives, William B. Kent, left Seattle for Oakland immediately. The case jumped back into high gear when police in both cities soon announced a search for a supposed accomplice, a man named Phoenix Markham.

Clara, meanwhile, seemed cheerful and eagerly gave reporters her opinions on various subjects. She talked about her many friends in Oakland and how she had earned all her money by working as a stenographer. She did not think she needed a lawyer and could not afford one anyway. She would not say anything about the murder, except to say, "I'll get out of it all right. I've got to."[2] She teased her captors for not catching her sooner, claiming that she had been hiding in plain sight.

When Detective Kent arrived in Oakland, he used the "best friend" approach with Clara. He escorted her out of jail, took her out to lunch, and then on a stroll through a park, during which reporters observed them having a very serious talk. The pair returned to the jail late in the afternoon. Kent wrote down a statement based on their conversation and Clara signed it.

Her story quickly made its way into the headlines. She told Kent that shortly after she and her mother moved in with Ferdinand, when she was only fourteen, Ferdinand had attacked her in the basement of the house. She fought him off and told her mother. Emma tried to smooth things over in order to "avoid notoriety" and they continued living with him for another five years. At some point, Emma gave Ferdinand $4,000 to invest for her.

> During this time I became acquainted with Mr. Winborn, who was a barber and married. There was nothing wrong about our acquaintance, but old Hochbrunn became jealous and attempted to prevent my seeing Mr. Winborn. Some heated words were passed and I decided to leave the Hochbrunn home, and told my mother she could leave with me or stay, just as she pleased. Mother decided to go with me, and we went to live on Harrison St. I think the number was 15.
>
> While we were living there, Mrs. Winborn called at our home. This was in 1918. It was her intention, I learned later, to kill me, but she was not successful. However, she did kill my mother and wounded me in the hip and then turned the gun on herself and ended her own life.[3]

Clara said she contacted Ferdinand after Winborn's death because she wanted her mother's investment back. Ferdinand sent her a ticket and she returned to Seattle on July 31, 1921.

> When I arrived at the home the room which I had formerly occupied was not fitted up for occupancy. The only room was the one which Hochbrunn occupied. He wanted me to live there with him, but I refused and finally fixed up my own room.
>
> About the first of September 1921, Hochbrunn appeared in my room entirely nude and made advances toward me. We had a battle during which a hair brush was my only weapon. I was able to beat him off, and I left the house at once and went to live with my cousin, Mrs. Clark, at 906 20th av., Seattle.[4]

On several occasions afterward, she returned to the apartment to collect things and to try to get her mother's investment back. In late September, she obtained a gun permit and purchased a revolver to protect herself. On October 12 or 13, she went back to the apartment to collect more of her possessions from her room. Ferdinand came into the room.

> He made improper proposals to me, and when I refused to listen to him, he became rough.
>
> He treated me frightfully, and I reached into the grip and pulled out the gun, which was wrapped in a newspaper. I told him it was a gun, and that I would kill him if he attacked me. He called me vile names, and in a scuffle he got the gun away from me. Later he lost possession of it, and I clinched with him and got the gun while we were kneeling in this position on the floor.
>
> I tried to get my hand under his so as to get him off his balance and shove him away, but he had his hand behind him, and I could not reach it. I had the gun, and I placed my arm back of him as we clinched there on the floor, and with my thumb I pulled the trigger, and the bullet entered the back of his head.[5]

Clara stated that she only told her story because of the kindness of Detective Kent. She also admitted she had forged the letters and telegrams to von Tobel.

Meanwhile, back in Seattle, Lieutenant. W. E. Justus was working on a first-degree murder case against her. Mrs. Robert R. Herbert, the wife of a Seattle detective, set out for Oakland to take charge of Clara during the journey home, which they would make by steamer.

The police were still searching for Clara's supposed accomplice, Markham, although reports surfaced that she had a fiancé—a different man—back in Kalamazoo, Michigan. The man's name was Raymond Herron and he worked as a telegraph operator. In the days immediately after Ferdinand's assumed date of death, Clara had wired him $250. A cryptic note accompanying the wire to Herron caused a great deal of speculation in the press:

> "Mark here," said the telegram. "Everything practically settled. No more saving a half cake of chocolate for tomorrow's lunch. This is the first of my very own money to spend. May I send Jigadere some of Ollie's clothes? Buy Maxine a new top and yourself a drink. Am going to order car from here for drive away in spring. Know agent here and want him to get commission. Wire me immediately. Love, Betty."[6]

Some speculated that the mysterious "Mark" referred to Phoenix Markham, the elusive "accomplice." Clara, however, denied there was any man involved, that it was entirely a matter of self-defense.

Although she did not explain much of anything, Clara enjoyed speaking to the press and did so frequently during this period. She talked to one reporter about her general views on life, explaining that she was a student of "Oriental philosophy." "Lying here at night I close my eyes and go wherever I care to. I wander over the hills and I don't feel that I am here at all. I have done that all my life."[7] She also announced that her name was actually Beatrice, and that she liked to make up names. She continued to insist that she did not need a lawyer. "I don't believe a jury will hang a girl for defending her honor."[8] However, eventually she did allow the court to appoint an attorney for her.

When Clara arrived back in Seattle with her two escorts, members of the press and law enforcement officials were waiting at Pier "D" to greet her. Vivid descriptions of the fetching young lady appeared on the front page of the *Seattle Star*:

> Quietly and becomingly gowned, Miss Skarin was by far the most attractive passenger to come off the ship. She seemed entirely at her ease and turned and waved as a battery of cameras were directed toward her.
>
> She didn't seem to be aware of the existence of the crowds that pushed around her as she walked to the sheriff's automobile. Her air was nothing less than regal. A slight smile on her lips, she climbed into the waiting car just as if she were a society leader, leaving the opera house.[9]

She later gushed to reporters about how glad she was to be back home in Seattle with its lovely hills, and described how delightful the steamer *Alexander* was, "just like a first-class hotel."

After meetings with the prosecutors, she went to her cell at city jail. The next day, police finally admitted that they now believed there was no such person as Phoenix Markham. This admission aided her defense, as it supported her story of shooting Ferdinand in self-defense during a violent struggle.

She did, however, tell police that a male accomplice had assisted her after the fact, helping her forge the letters to von Tobel and robbing Ferdinand's pockets and trunk. She said these actions were not her idea but the idea of her accomplice, whom she refused to identify. She said her accomplice had hidden Ferdinand's body with the blanket so she would not have to see him while they cut open his pockets to retrieve the keys to his trunk. Tellingly, she claimed that she and the accomplice had forged the letters "in his office," and that the man had taken a lot of papers from Ferdinand's trunk, as well as the hoard of gold coins.

Clara also explained the mysterious "Mark," from the telegram to Raymond Herron in Kalamazoo. She said that Mark Ten Suie, a Chinese, wanted to adopt her, and had given her some money.[10] Mark Ten Suie was a well-known Seattle silk merchant. Attorney John Dore took Clara's case, and on September 23, 1922, she pleaded not guilty to charges of capital murder. On that same day, in a strange turn of events perhaps known to Clara or perhaps not, her so-called fiancé, Raymond Herron of Kalamazoo, Michigan, married another woman.

After some delays, Clara Skarin's capital murder trial began on January 9, 1923. John Dore had rounded up a number of witnesses who were eager to testify to Ferdinand's bad character, including tales of his rip-off schemes in the real estate business and stories about his bad temper and jealous nature. Dore's opening statement was a shocker: He declared that after poor, frightened Clara had shot Ferdinand in self-defense, she had been manipulated into robbing him by Ferdinand's own attorney, Edward von Tobel. Dore said that von Tobel urged Clara to flee, preferably to Brazil, and that von Tobel had kept most of the loot for himself. As evidence, Dore presented documents showing that von Tobel had deposited $1,760 in gold into his personal bank around the time of the murder.

Von Tobel later took the stand in his own defense, explaining that the gold had nothing to do with Ferdinand, and that it was related to the settlement of an estate in Austria. He said he had had no contact with Clara during the period when Ferdinand first disappeared and he had gone to see her in November to ask her where Hochbrunn was. He presented a telegram to him, signed by Clara, that said Ferdinand was ill and heading to California. He told the courtroom that he had known Clara since 1909 and that she had completely deceived him. Von Tobel was never charged with any crime and was entirely exonerated by the sheriff's office.

Two local telegraph office managers testified for the prosecution that within two days of Ferdinand's death, Clara had bought money transfers, paying for them in gold. She told one of the operators that her uncle had died and left her $20,000.

Clara took the stand and told her story. Prosecutors asked her to read one of the telegrams she had sent to Raymond Herron, which contained a muddled series of fables about a white girl kidnapped and shipped off to China, a murdered Dutchman, holdup men killing someone, and a girl called "C.E.S." murdered in San Francisco's Chinatown.

> "B.W." said the yellow note, had disappeared, adding, "we are trying to create the impression that C.E.S. was B.W. That's a good idea. Let it ride. Know nothing. Destroy this." The note was signed a friend.[11]

It could be assumed that B. W. is Betty Winborn and C. E. S. is Clara E. Skarin, and that these were proposed cover stories designed to explain the disappearance of Betty, or Clara, or perhaps the Dutchman. It is not clear whether anyone in the packed courtroom was able to follow this narrative.

Clara admitted to the court that she had spent time in the apartment while Ferdinand lay dead in another room. She shuffled around, successfully giving the impression to the Chedotals downstairs that Ferdinand was walking around in his slippers.

The trial lasted five days. During closing arguments, her second defense attorney, John J. Sullivan, reviewed the harrowing life of his client and the horrifying attacks that Ferdinand had made on Clara. "Down south they lynch men who do the things to little girls and women that this beast did to this little girl when she was a child of 14 years," he yelled.[12] One female juror wept, and another had tears in her eyes.

The jury was out for two and a half hours, during which time they took three ballots. On the third, they reached a unanimous verdict: Clara Skarin/ Betty Winborn/Betty Parrish/Beatrice was not guilty.

After the trial ended and Clara was set free, she announced she would likely return to her life in Oakland, where "Betty Parrish" had so many friends. She also reminded reporters of her special way of viewing the events of her life:

"Thirteen is my lucky number," Miss Skarin remarked, recalling that she killed Hochbrunn on October 13 two years ago. "When I was arrested in Oakland, they put me on the 13th floor of the jail. The number of this courtroom is 313 and the room in which the jury reached its verdict was 313-A."[13]

19

Massacre at Erland's Point (1934)

It was the strange case of the dogs barking in the night that finally caught the attention, and annoyance, of Tom Sanders. The racket came from his neighbor's home in Erland's Point, overlooking Ostrich Bay in Kitsap County. The dogs had been barking for several days. Finally, he and another neighbor, K. Erland, decided to march over to the Flieder place and make it stop. It was Saturday night, March 31, 1934.

When they arrived, they found three French poodles trapped in a large Packard parked in front of the house. The Packard did not belong to their neighbors, Frank and Anna Flieder, who did not own any dogs either. The men knocked on the door, but no one answered, so they let the dogs out of the car and gave them food and water.

Tom Sanders knew Frank and Anna well enough to have the phone number of Frank's brother, Louis, so he gave him a call. Louis became alarmed and asked Tom to investigate further. The two men prowled around the house, this time knocking on the kitchen door. Again, they got no answer.

Finally, Sanders noticed a living room window had the blinds partly up, so he peered in, sweeping his flashlight across the dark room. What his narrow beam of light revealed was a scene as horrific as the notorious Clutter family massacre, made famous by Truman Capote in his book *In Cold Blood*. Sanders rushed home and called the Kitsap County Sheriff's Office.

Sheriff Daniel Blankenship arrived with several deputies, and they broke into the house. Inside, each room presented a new shock.

In the dining room, a man sat at a card table, a pile of playing cards and poker chips in front of him. A pair of glasses and an empty wallet lay on the table, along with two other piles of cards. The man in the chair was bound, gagged, and slumped to one side. Opposite him, crumpled under the card table and leaning against a day bed was a woman. She was not bound but marks showed on her wrists. She was almost curled into a fetal position, with one arm propped upon the day bed. Both the man and the woman had been shot in the head. Both were dead.

The living room had been the scene of a ferocious battle, and two men lay on the floor. One was facing down, his hands bound behind his back. Someone had smashed his head in. The other was not bound and had obviously put up a mighty struggle. In a death grip, he clutched the leg of an overturned coffee table. The killer had pummeled his face beyond recognition. Next to his body lay a bloody claw hammer.

In a bedroom, deputies found a woman dead on the bed. Identified as Anna Flieder, her eyes were covered with tape and she was bound and gagged. The killer had stabbed her in the chest with a kitchen knife. The drawer of her bedside table was open and had been ransacked. In the bedroom closet they found yet another dead man, whose throat had been cut.

In total, deputies discovered six murder victims in the Flieder home— two women and four men. The house was in a shambles, ransacked by the killer or killers. They had left several weapons at the scene, including the claw hammer, a blackjack, a stove poker, and two large knives. Deputies did not find a gun. It was clear that the killings had occurred at least a couple of days earlier.

Sheriff Blankenship understood that he was not equipped to manage such a massive investigation, so he left his deputies to guard the crime scene and took the ferry to Seattle to get help. He particularly wanted the aid of Seattle's famed "Sherlock Holmes," Luke May. May was a pioneer in forensic science and was called in on most of the region's big cases during the 1920s and '30s. He ran his own forensics lab and specialized in toolmark evidence. In 1922, he had invented the "Revelarescope," a specialized double-lensed magnascope that allowed the lab to compare two objects for a possible match, such as toolmarks on two different surfaces.

Meanwhile word of a mass murder spread, and a large crowd gathered outside the home. A rumor later circulated that at least one of the deputies guarding the murder scene "charged a crowd of 150 people 25 cents each to walk through the house and view the slaughter. The gawkers scattered gum wrappers and one woman stole the stockings off Anna Flieder's legs."[1]

When Luke May arrived on April 1, Easter morning, the crowd of onlookers, reporters and press photographers was already on scene. During May's initial inspection, he made several critical observations that would have an important bearing on the case: first, he declared that at least one killer had been injured in the battle. He determined this by noting that there was a considerable amount of blood and broken glass in the kitchen, but none of the victims were found in that room. The broken glass was also bloody, but none of the victims had injuries that matched the glass fragments.

He thus surmised that the blood belonged to the killer and that the injury was fairly significant.

He also noted that several Wednesday newspapers were present in the home but no Thursday papers. He deduced that the killings had probably occurred on Wednesday, March 28. Another point that would prove significant was that the killers had bound some of the victims with ice skate laces.

Police soon identified the six victims. Face down on the living room floor with his hands bound was Frank Flieder, forty-five, the owner of the home. He was a retired grocer of considerable means who came from a wealthy Bremerton family. His third wife, Anna, around fifty, was dead in the bedroom. She was the former Anna Taylor, widow of a prominent druggist. She and Frank Flieder had been married for less than two and a half years. They were known in the area for being "party people" who entertained often. Anna possessed a number of valuable jewels, which were missing from the home.

The other man found dead in the living room was clearly the one who had wriggled out of his binds and fought back. He died while gripping the leg of a broken coffee table. Authorities identified him as Eugene Chenevert, thirty-eight, of Bremerton. He was a retired entertainer and singer who had gone by the stage name of Bert Vincent. His wife was Peggy Chenevert, thirty—the woman found crumpled beneath the card table and shot in the head. She was the other half of the stage duo known as Bert and Peggy Vincent. The Packard and three French poodles belonged to the Cheneverts. Peggy had also apparently escaped from her binds but was shot before she could get away.

The man slumped in his chair at the card table was Magnus Jordan, fifty, a retired navy man who lived nearby. Finally, the dead man found in the closet was Fred Bolcom, a bartender at a local beer parlor.

Investigators immediately began questioning neighbors, friends, and family of the deceased. Locals had seen the Packard arrive at the house on Monday and the Flieders had been spotted at the house earlier in the week. Several neighbors reported seeing the Flieders as late as Thursday afternoon. A local bartender said he had sold beer to Chenevert on Thursday. Three men were seen racing away in a car on Thursday night. Based on this testimony, detectives disregarded Luke May's suggestion that the killings occurred Wednesday night and settled on Thursday as the night of the crimes.

This turned out to be a wrong assumption that led them astray for many months, as they discounted critical clues based on the timing. One important statement came from a Bremerton shipyard worker said he had encountered an injured man on the ferry from Bremerton to Seattle. The man's face was cut and bruised, and he wore a hastily constructed bandage on his head. Yet the witness was certain he had seen the man early Thursday morning, before the presumed night of the killings.

Another report came in from two Bremerton men, who claimed that a local waitress had come to their home in the early hours of the morning in a disheveled state, missing a heel off one of her shoes. This interested detectives because they had found the heel of a woman's shoe outside the Flieder residence. They located the waitress and questioned her. She told them she had been out with a sailor who attacked her, and that she had needed to jump out of his car. Detectives did not press her on this story because the witnesses insisted that it had happened on Wednesday night or the early hours of Thursday, before the killings.

During the following weeks and months, police followed up dozens of clues and pursued numerous suspects. They fixated for a time on a man who had recently moved to Idaho, who had been seen there with severe head lacerations. The man had appeared in pictures found in Chenevert's home, dancing with Mrs. Flieder. His "swarthy complexion" was apparently also cause for suspicion. He turned out to have an alibi and was eliminated as a suspect.

Meanwhile, Luke May's team lifted every fingerprint they could find in the home. He had devised a new method for analyzing prints that were hard to discern because the skin oil had dried. Many of the prints he found did not belong to the six victims, and those he distributed to agencies across the country, hoping for a match with known criminals.

In November 1935, about eight months into the investigation, Sheriff Daniel L. Blankenship died in a car accident. His brother, Deputy Sheriff Rush Blankenship, took over his dead brother's job and duties. It was election time and Rush ran for sheriff and won. Shortly after, Luke May received word of a match to one of the fingerprint cards he had sent out. Kansas officials identified a fingerprint from the house as belonging to Rush Blankenship, an ex-convict who had served a term in Kansas for issuing bad checks. A third Blankenship brother, Walton, had joined up with Rush's opponent in the election and made the information public. This disqualified Rush's election victory. Rumors circulated that Rush responded by beating up Walton.

Meanwhile, the ghastly murder case continued to languish. Months became a year, and then a year and a half had passed with no viable leads. Seattle officials offered a $500 reward (about $9,300 in current dollars) for information leading to the arrest of the killer or killers.

Finally, in October 1935, eighteen months after the slayings at Erland's Point, investigators caught a major break. Seattle police arrested a petty criminal and ex-con, Larry Paulos, for robbery. Paulos, eager to make a deal for himself, told detectives he had information about the Erland Point murders. He said his wife, whom he had married about a month earlier, knew something about the Erland Point murders as well as the murder of a special investigator in Portland named W. Frank Akin.

Police soon discovered that Larry Paulos' bride, Peggy, was the same waitress they had questioned earlier about losing her heel. When they brought her in, Peggy Paulos denied her husband's story and was released. However, Peggy had second thoughts and appeared later at the offices of a former congressman, Attorney Ralph A. Horr. There, she gave a detailed statement about her involvement in the murders. Horr immediately took the information to the police, who brought her in for another interview.

Peggy Paulos quickly corrected a critical assumption about the murders that had contributed to the lack of progress in the investigation—Luke May had been correct about the timing of the massacre. The victims had been killed Wednesday night, not Thursday night. She also told police that all six victims had been murdered by one killer, an ex-convict named Leo Hall. She told them that she feared for her life, now that her husband had revealed her role in the case. She thought Hall would try to kill her because she knew too much.

Police kept Peggy in custody while launching a search for Leo Hall. Portland detectives working on the Akin case soon found and arrested him. After a predictable struggle over who would try Leo Hall first, Washington State prevailed and escorted Hall to jail there. Detectives brought in the dock worker who had described seeing the injured man on the ferry early on Thursday morning. The worker identified Leo Hall as the man he saw. It also emerged that Hall had once worked at a skating rink, which provided a circumstantial link to the skating laces used to bind the victims.

Kitsap County authorities indicted Leo Hall for the murders of six people. They also charged Peggy Paulos with murder. Both pleaded innocent. Before the trial began, word spread about a gang of vigilantes planning a lynching, so deputies moved Hall to the Thurston County jail.

Prosecutors decided to try the two together for the murder of Eugene Chenevert, to be held in the Port Orchard courtroom of Judge H. G. Sutton. The prosecution asked for the death penalty for thirty-three-year-old Leo Hall but not for Peggy Paulos, who would be testifying as their star witness.

As the date of the trial approached, local diners stocked up on extra provisions in anticipation of the enormous crowds expected for the sensational trial.

Once the trial began, the jury was soon seated, consisting of eight men and four women. The courtroom, as expected, was packed. One of the first witnesses for the prosecution was a Seattle doctor who had stitched up an injury to Leo Hall's head shortly after the killings. The prosecution also escorted the entire jury to the Flieder house and gave them a tour of the murder scene.

A former girlfriend of Leo Hall's, Carrie Stickles, travelled from Tennessee to testify against him. She presented a letter he had written her immediately after the killings, asking her for money so he could come to Tennessee to be with her. She read the letter to the courtroom, much of which was printed by the local press:

> Darling, this time I am writing to you and you don't know what anguish it is causing me to do so.
>
> I am in a jam, Carrie, a frightful mess and need you to stand by me.
>
> I couldn't bring myself to confide in any other woman, but I feel you have the strength of character and purpose to bear with me like a good soldier.
>
> An attempt was made on my life. I was totally unsuspecting and am still puzzled as to the purpose. Our friend that removed your tonsils (Dr. W.M. MacWhinnie, Seattle physician and surgeon) put 24 stitches in my head.
>
> I've got to get out of here somehow immediately and secretly.[2]

Carrie Stickles did not send Leo Hall any money.

The courtroom grew quiet when twenty-seven-year-old Peggy Paulos came to the stand. She had been Hall's girlfriend. Her attorney presented her as a simple girl who had been manipulated and intimidated by the handsome and powerful Hall, a former boxer. She came from a poor family in the mountains of West Virginia, whose father had later worked on a "stump farm" near Enumclaw, Washington. Peggy's young life had grown more difficult with the death of her father and the breakup of her family.

A pitiable story also emerged, possibly spread by her attorney, that Peggy's husband, Larry, had written her from jail to say he wanted a divorce. He jeered at her for sending him money and writing him love letters, which he had shown to his fellow inmates.

On the stand, she told the courtroom that she was acquainted with Anna Flieder and had told Leo Hall about Anna's jewelry collection. Hall decided that he wanted to stage a robbery and insisted that Peggy accompany him. The pair of them stopped at Hall's bank, where he removed a pearl-handled .32 revolver from a safe deposit box. They took the ferry from Seattle to Bremerton and arrived at the Flieder house at 11:30 p.m. Before entering the house, they put on masks and gloves, then knocked on the kitchen door.

When someone opened the door, they burst in and told them it was a "stick up." At that point, there were only four people in the house—Mrs. and Mrs. Flieder, Anna Chenevert, and Fred Bolcom. Hall kept them covered with the revolver while Peggy tied their hands with skating lace and gagged them with adhesive tape. A short time later, Chenevert and Jordan arrived, carrying a box of beer. Peggy then tied them up using torn strips of bedsheets.

According to Peggy's testimony, as the intruders searched the house for jewels and money, Anna Flieder told them she was sick and needed to lie down. It is not clear how she could speak when gagged. Hall took her into the bedroom. When Anna lay down on the bed, Hall stabbed her with a carving knife. Peggy testified that he came back from the bedroom with blood on him.

He then took Fred Bolcom into the bedroom, where he murdered him by hitting him over the head with a fireplace poker.

At this point, Peggy fled the scene. Hall screamed at her and fired the gun at her, but he missed and she ran away. This detail was corroborated by a bullet founded embedded in one of the doors. She lost her heel during the flight and did not know how or when Hall killed the others.

She said she saw Hall again in Seattle a few days later, and he told her he had killed the others as well. She asked him why, and he said that one of them had recognized her (likely Anna Flieder, whom she had known) and that "dead witnesses can't talk." He told her that Chenevert had broken loose and there had been a violent struggle, during which Chenevert hit him over the head with a beer bottle. Chenevert had suffered twenty-two blows with the claw hammer, mostly to his skull.

Peggy insisted during her testimony that Hall had forced her to go along to the robbery and that she had been terrified when he began killing the people. She said when she saw Hall later, he threatened to kill her if she talked.

On cross-examination, Hall's defense attorney, Everett Butts, suggested that Peggy had made up the whole story in hopes of freeing her husband from jail. He asked her if she had been given immunity for her testimony, which she denied. He insisted that she demonstrate how she had bound the wrists of Frank Flieder, which she did, using Butts as the "victim." In all, about twenty witnesses testified for the prosecution, mostly corroborating aspects of Peggy's testimony.

At several junctures, Everett Butts moved for a mistrial, but each move was denied by Judge Sutton. When Hall's defense began, Butts called five witnesses who testified that they had seen one or more of the victims, alive and well, the day after the supposed killings. Hall's mother and siblings testified that Hall had been at his mother's home on the night of the killings.

Hall also testified on his own behalf. He explained his head injury, saying he had been caught up in a barroom brawl, during which he hit a man over the head with a chair. He later heard that the man had a fractured skull and might die, and so he had written the letter to Carrie Sickles in hopes of leaving the state to avoid possible charges in that incident.

Hall remained calm during most of his testimony but lost his composure when pressed aggressively by Special Prosecutor Ray. R. Greenwood during cross-examination. He also refused to answer several questions from Peggy's attorney, Ralph Horr. Horr did not present a case for the defense of Peggy Paulos, instead relying on her testimony on behalf of the prosecution that she had acted under duress.

After ten days of testimony, the case went to the jury. They returned with a verdict on December 19: Leo Hall was convicted of first-degree murder.

Peggy Paulos was freed. On December 23, the court sentenced Leo Hall to death by hanging.

Hall's attorney requested a new trial, which was denied. His appeals succeeded in delaying the death warrant for a number of months. The following spring, the State Supreme Court heard the case. In April, by unanimous decree, the court upheld the conviction and death sentence. A petition by Butts for a rehearing of the appeal was denied. Hall's execution was set for September 11, 1936.

On that day, his mother, who had travelled to Walla Walla, was allowed in to say goodbye to her son. Some 125 witnesses were on hand to view the black hood being placed over Hall's head. On September 11, 1936, at 11 p.m., Leo Hall died by hanging. Witnesses reported a smile on his face.

Peggy Paulos was said to have received death threats after the verdict, and she told friends that she meant to return home to West Virginia. King County Sheriff William Severyns announced that the $500 reward would go to inmate Larry Paulos.

20

A Tale of Two Kidnappings (1935)

The headline on the front page of the *Seattle Star* on May 25, 1935, read "Weyerhaeuser Family Demands Secrecy." It was not clear how the "secret" got out, but there probably was not a soul in Tacoma who did not know by the end of the day that nine-year-old George Weyerhaeuser had been kidnapped.

The Weyerhaeuser family was well-known throughout the United States, famed for their vast timber holdings in the West and Midwest, with a fabulous fortune of over a billion dollars ($18 billion in 2018 money). George was the son of John Philip Weyerhaeuser, Jr., and the grandson of John Phillip, Sr., the patriarch, who had just died a week before. The kidnappers had chosen their target well.

Young George had disappeared the previous day after leaving the Lowell School at lunchtime. His routine was to walk over to the Annie Wright Seminary where his sister Ann was a student. The two children were always met there by the family chauffeur, who whisked them off to a meal at home.

On that Friday, George did not show up to meet his sister. Still, the family was not alarmed until George failed to return to school after lunch. They launched a search. The only sighting of the boy came from a young lad on street crossing duty, who had seen George leave the school at lunch.

On Friday night around dinnertime, a ransom note arrived at the family mansion by special motorcycle messenger from the post office. This information also made its way into the papers. Despite the family's plea for secrecy, FBI director J. Edgar Hoover announced that FBI agents were on the case. Reporters who camped out in front of the Weyerhaeuser home described a procession of people and automobiles in and out of the place. Volunteers from throughout Tacoma mobilized to search, including taxi drivers and George's fellow students. Rumors circulated about a tan sedan and several men who had been seen lurking around the school.

Details about the ransom note emerged. It was signed by "The Egoist" and instructed the family to post ads in the *Seattle Daily Post-Intelligencer* signed by "Percy Minnie." "The Egoist" wanted $200,000 in unmarked, used bills, in specific denominations. They instructed the family not to notify authorities and threatened to kill the young boy. Police and federal agents had already been involved for several hours by the time the family received the ransom note.

Investigators called in noted Seattle criminologist Luke S. May to examine the note for fingerprints, though it was not clear whether he found any. It was long and typewritten, with George's signature scrawled on the back of the envelope.

The family followed instructions, placing two ads in the *Post-Intelligencer*. One read "Expect to be ready to come Monday. Answer, Percy Minnie." The other said: "Due to publicity beyond our control please indicate another method of reaching you. Hurry, relieve anguished mother. Percy Minnie."[1]

While the family waited for a reply, speculation filled newspapers across the country. Lumbermen in Oregon were striking at the time and some wondered if the kidnapping might be related. Others insisted that famed mobsters, Machine Gun Kelly and Alvin Karpis, must be behind it. Reports of a similar-looking boy led authorities on wild goose chases to Canada and Port Angeles. Police rushed to an abandoned house a mile away from the mansion when someone reported a banging noise there. Eight officers forced their way in to find a loose window clanking in the wind.

The kidnapping and murder of baby Charles Lindbergh, Jr., had happened only three years before and was still fresh in everyone's mind. A Chicago psychiatrist declared that "Egoist" would be homicidal if trapped.[2]

The Weyerhaeusers had three other children: Ann, thirteen; Phillip, ten; and Elizabeth, two. After a second ransom note arrived, the family hastened the kids out of the house to stay with relatives. On Wednesday, May 29, George's father, John Phillip, was absent from the home, leading to wild speculation that the pay-off was in the works.

In fact, a family friend had followed instructions from the ransom note: he drove a car to a rendezvous location and left the car there with the money inside. As he walked away, someone jumped into the car and drove it away.

At 4 a.m. on June 1, an Issaquah farmer was startled by a knock at the door. It was raining. The sun would not come up for another hour. When the farmer opened the door, he found a young boy, cold and wet. The boy told him his name was George Weyerhaeuser.

The kindly farmer, Louis Bonifas, brought him inside, dried him off, warmed him up, and fed him. George had no shoes, so Louis loaned him an ill-fitting pair belonging to his daughter. Louis did not have a phone so he would have to crank up his old car in order to drive George back to his family.

Once the sun came up, the two of them set off to find the Tacoma police station. At Renton, they stopped for gas and tried to call the Weyerhaeuser home but could not get through. Louis called the police, who immediately set out to meet them.

A reporter for the *Seattle Times*, John H. Dreher, apparently had a source within the Tacoma Police Department who told him what was happening. He hired a taxi and somehow intercepted Louis and George before the police did. It was not clear how he convinced Louis to pull over—perhaps by posing as a police officer. He then convinced Louis to let him take George home to his parents.

During the taxi ride, Dreher interviewed young George. The interview constituted a massive scoop for Dreher that he published in the *Seattle Times* and which was reprinted widely in papers across the country. Dreher directed the taxi driver to take a circuitous route so he had more time with the young kidnap victim. Dreher also suggested to George that he lie back on the seat while Dreher hunkered down on the floor of the taxi—presumably so that police would not spot them.

He justified his actions by describing the mayhem that would have besieged the poor boy at the police station. Positing himself as a hero for saving George from that horror, he produced an article full of exclamations such as "Gosh, his face was dirty," and much gushing about how George was "bubbling over." He also got Louis Bonifas's name wrong. Dreher even asked the lad to give him a kiss, a detail that he included in his story.[3]

It emerged that the kidnappers had abandoned George in the woods, apparently without shoes, late on Friday night. The child had walked 6 miles through the rain and dark, looking for someone to help him. The people at one farmhouse turned him away before he came to the farm of the Bonifas family, who rescued him.

Later, George's grateful father offered Louis Bonifas a job at the Snoqualmie Falls Lumber Mill, which he accepted. Weyerhaeuser also gave Louis enough money to purchase several acres of land and build his family a new house at Snoqualmie. Many decades later, when George was in his nineties, an interviewer asked him about the kidnapping. He had forgotten most of the details, explaining that his parents thought it was better for him that they did not dwell on it. The family therefore avoided the subject. All those years later, he had no memory of Dreher the reporter, but he did remember the good-hearted farmer who took him in and helped him.

As soon as George was home safe, the search for the kidnappers kicked into high gear. Police distributed the serial numbers of the bank notes across the country. George told officers that on the day he was taken, he was walking to meet his sister and had just climbed a flight of steps when two men approached him at the top. One asked him directions to Stadium Way.

He said he did not know, and the man asked, "Why so shy?" Then both men grabbed him, covered his mouth, and stuffed him into the trunk of a sedan. He said they often kept him blindfolded during his captivity. For a time, they confined him in a hole in the ground. Later, they moved him to a house.

On June 9, the first reports came in about a woman in Salt Lake City passing the ransom notes. Other reports came from Minnesota. After more than twenty of the notes had been used in Salt Lake City, the search for the kidnappers focused there.

Soon, clerks in a ten-cent store and a market zeroed in on the woman who had been using the notes. The woman, identified as a blonde wearing a "house dress," would offer a larger bill such as a five in payment for a small purchase. Police stationed officers nearby in case she returned.

On a Saturday morning, the woman appeared at one of the stores and passed a $5 bill to a clerk. The clerk called the cash girl, who took it to the cashier where they checked it for the serial number. It was identified as one of the ransom bills. Two officers immediately arrested her. Detective W. M. Rogers and Patrolman L. B. Gifford hauled her off to the local federal offices and handed her over to FBI agents.

Nineteen-year-old Mrs. Margaret Waley did not last long under FBI grilling. She soon confessed that her husband, Harmon Waley, and another man, William Mahan, had kidnapped George Weyerhaeuser. She insisted that she had only found out about it after the fact. She told them where they could find her husband.

Agents quickly arrested Harmon Waley, a petty crook with a long criminal record. At age twenty-four, he had already been arrested seven times, starting his career as a teen in Aberdeen, Washington when he landed in reform school for burglary. Other prior charges included more burglaries, grand larceny, robbery, auto theft, and parole violations.

The Waleys wasted no time in telling police that the real mastermind behind the kidnapping was thirty-four-year-old William Mahan.

Meanwhile, in Butte, Montana, a patrol officer pulled over a man he recognized—an ex-con named William Dainard, who was well-known to the police. To the officer's surprise, as he approached Dainard's car, the man suddenly jumped out and bolted on foot. The officer tried to catch him, but an unidentified bulldog intervened.

Once he got the bulldog off him, the officer discovered why Dainard had panicked. Inside the car, he found a huge cache of money. In all, he found $15,000 dollars from the Weyerhaeuser kidnapping case. It turned out that William Dainard was William Mahan.

Back in Salt Lake City, Margaret and Harmon Waley, after considerable questioning, led agents to a secret stash in Emigration Canyon, famed for being the place where Brigham Young first entered the original site of Salt

Lake City. There, officers dug up what remained of the Waley's share of the kidnapping loot: $90,700.

Margaret Waley's grandfather, Julius Thulin of Ogden, was soon telling the press how his granddaughter had married the wrong fellow and that she had never been in trouble before. The Thulins were a prominent Mormon family and were extremely upset about Margaret's activities, especially the fact that she had brought the criminals into her grandfather's house. Julius Thulin would later testify in court how Margaret and her cronies had arrived at his home, each carrying a suitcase, presumably full of ransom money. Police soon also identified a house at 1509 W. Eleventh Street in Spokane where George had been kept during his captivity.

While he continued to elude capture, William Mahan/Dainard was dubbed by Hoover's FBI as public enemy number one. Like Waley, he had a long criminal record, including auto theft and bank robbery.

Harmon Waley pleaded guilty to kidnapping charges and on June 20, less than a month after the crime, he was sentenced to forty-five years. He was sent to the federal penitentiary at McNeil Island, then later transferred to Alcatraz.

Margaret Waley also pleaded guilty, but the judge refused to accept her plea. What ensued was a strange tussle between the parties, in which Margaret continued to insist that she was guilty, but the judge continued to insist that she could not be guilty since she did not know about the kidnapping until afterward.

Unlike Harmon, Margaret ended up having a jury trial. Her defense attorney told the judge that Margaret had a mentality that was lower than that of the child they had kidnapped. The attorney also argued that she was young, had been subject to threats from Dainard, and was operating under the influence of Harmon Waley.

The prosecution accused her of driving Dainard to the spot where he picked up the ransom. They pointed out that she had done nothing to make life easier for George and that she showed no remorse.

On July 13, her case went to the jury, who came back with a guilty verdict. The judge sentenced her to twenty years. While her attorney tried to angle for a new trial, she insisted she was satisfied with the verdict, stating that the sentence would "make it easier waiting for Harmon." She was sent to the Federal Women's Detention Farm at Milan, Michigan. "Now every day will bring me nearer to Harmon," she said.[4]

Almost a year later, authorities in San Francisco were following a long trail of bills from the Weyerhaeuser ransom. On May 8, 1936, agents spotted William Dainard parking his car and they closed in. He gave up without a fight. He was carrying $7,300 on his person and they found another $13,000 in a zippered bag in the car. A considerable portion of the bills seized were from the ransom, though he had tried to alter the serial numbers. Washington authorities brought him back and he pleaded guilty to kidnapping and conspiracy. The court sentenced him to sixty years. Like Waley, he served a few years at McNeil Island and then was transferred to Alcatraz.

After the capture of Dainard, reporters approached young George in the playground at his school and asked how he felt about the news. He assured them he was "sure glad."

In the 1950s, authorities transferred Waley and Dainard to the U.S. Penitentiary in Marion, Illinois. Both were eventually released. Meanwhile, Margaret had given up waiting for Harmon. After serving a partial sentence, she remarried another man in 1953.

About six months after authorities captured and imprisoned Dainard, kidnappers targeted the same Tacoma neighborhood. The trouble began at Haddaway Hall, an enormous mansion that was previously the home of John Phillip Weyerhaeuser, Sr., near the home of his son, John Phillip, Jr. After the elder Weyerhaeuser died, Mr. and Mrs. Franklin purchased the mansion. On November 24, 1936, a prowler climbed an 18-foot ladder and crawled through the window of the Franklin's six-year-old son. The child was sick at the time and his mother was sleeping in the room with her son. The intruder's flashlight beam landed on Mrs. Franklin. She woke up, screamed, grabbed her son, and ran from the room. The man escaped down the ladder.

The Franklins hired professional guards for the next several nights but soon replaced them with a sixteen-year-old boy. His job was to sleep in the home with a rifle. Two nights later, the family's maid spotted someone on the grounds. Before she could alert the family, the intruder brazenly punched a fist through glass in a door, waking up the entire household. He ran up the stairs, where the teenaged guard shot at him. The prowler returned fire but turned and left.

A few weeks later, a stranger targeted another household in the neighborhood. Two days after Christmas, a disheveled man appeared outside the French doors at the home of Dr. William and Hazel Mattson. In the living room were ten-year-old Charles Mattson, his fourteen-year-old sister, Muriel, and Muriel's friend, Alice Chatfield. The parents were out visiting with friends and had left the children in the care of sixteen-year-old William, who was asleep in his room.

The stranger waved a gun at the children, then broke the glass of the French doors and burst into the room. The girls screamed, which awoke William. The man dropped a note, grabbed the 70-lb Charles, and ran. Charles's spaniel puppy chased after him, nipping at his heels, but he disappeared down a terraced hillside.

Within an hour, federal agents and police swarmed the house, interviewing the children and installing special phone lines. Once again, the city of Tacoma mobilized a search for the missing boy.

The kidnapper had used toy print blocks and ink to create the note. It had been folded and re-folded multiple times and appeared to have been in the kidnapper's pocket for some time. It did not specifically name Charles but demanded $18,000 in return for "the boy." Investigators assumed this kidnapper was the same person who had entered Haddaway Hall and that the original target had been the Franklin's little boy.

Dr. Mattson was a prominent physician and surgeon, but not wealthy. Friends and relatives had to help him raise the ransom, which the note insisted would double each week if the transaction did not take place on a schedule.

Muriel and Alice told agents that the man was unshaven, swarthy, and roughly dressed, and that the things he said did not make much sense. He wore a mask at first, but it came off at some point. They said that after he ran off with Charles, they heard a car start.

As with the Weyerhaeuser case, rumors abounded, and police followed up numerous leads that went nowhere. Once again, a mob of reporters arrived quickly and camped out in front of the Mattson home. The press speculated wildly about what was going on and reported every movement of persons in and out of the house, including their moods and descriptions of them and their cars. Reporters even followed people as they left the house, hoping they might be headed to a rendezvous with the kidnappers, apparently heedless of the danger they created.

Per instructions from the note, the Mattsons placed an ad in the *Seattle Times* on December 29: "Mable: Please give us your address. Ann." Two days later, the kidnapper had not contacted the family. The family placed another ad in the *Times*, this time signing it differently: "Mabel: Please give us your address. Tim."

It emerged later that the note itself was not consistent about whether it should be signed Ann or Tim. It became clear that this kidnapper was "an amateur" and unstable. They based this conclusion on the small amount of money he demanded, the muddled message in the note, and the reckless way he took young Charles in front of witnesses. Experts warned that this made the kidnapper more dangerous, although the note did not include a death threat.

On December 31, the desperate family placed another ad, saying "We are ready," but by the next day, they were deeply worried that the kidnapping would not be resolved. They had been unable to contact the kidnapper and there had been no proof that Charles was okay.

On January 3, the contents of the note itself was leaked to the press and was published widely.

Get eighteen thousand dollars, five and ten dollar old bills, number not to run consecutively.

Get ten thousand in fifty dollar old bills, numbers not to run consecutively.

This amount will double each week.

The boy is safe.

When you are ready, insert in personal column of the Seattle Times— "Mable what is your address. Ann."

Disregard any notes received by you unless this type and color ink is used and signed Tim.

Use an old Ford car.

Tim.[5]

On January 4, the family placed yet another ad, but they still received no word from the kidnapper. They begged reporters to back off, stay away from the house, and stop publishing stories about the kidnapping. The papers cooperated.

On January 7 and 8, the family posted two more messages, trying to reassure the kidnappers: "I am getting the notes. Police are not intercepting them. I accept your method of identification. All requests have been carried out. I will do as instructed without anyone knowing."[6] On January 10, the Mattsons placed another desperate ad in the *Seattle Times*:

Mable—We are still waiting. All arrangements have been carried out in accordance with instructions contained in notes received. Be certain to give me information so that I may guard against imposters and hijackers, and be more specific in your instructions. In view of lapse of time also desire new proof my son is alive and well.—Ann.[7]

On Monday, January 11, a nineteen-year-old Everett lad was out hunting rabbits near his parents' farm. In a clump of snow-covered brush, he found the frozen and nude body of a young boy. The boy's head was crushed, his teeth were broken, and his entire body was bloody and bruised. Someone had stabbed him in the back with a long-bladed knife.

A Mattson family friend identified the body as Charles. The coroner determined that he had likely been killed Thursday or Friday, January 7 or 8. His killer had thrown him into a water-filled ditch until he was frozen, then moved him again and dumped him 150 feet from the Pacific Highway (Highway 99). Footprints indicated that a single person had carried him there. Before killing him, the murderer had kept him bound, tortured him, and carried him around in a car trunk. Authorities did not say for sure that the killer had sexually molested Charles, but his lack of clothes pointed in that direction.

A representative eventually released a statement from the shattered family:

The ransom definitely was not paid, although the doctor made many attempts to pay it. The kidnapper was too yellow to come out of his hiding to obtain the money.

Charles had been dead a long time, probably between three days and a week. When I identified his body today, the blood on his face was black and frozen.

The kidnapper communicated three times with Dr. Mattson by mail and telephone but no effort was made to trace the letters or calls for fear of endangering the safety of Charles.

The kidnapper has acted like a trout coming out of his lair, almost taking the bait, and crawling back into it again.

Dr. Mattson asked me to tell the newspaper boys we express our sincere appreciation for the way they have treated us, even though I at times have become a little vexatious at some of their stories.[8]

Word of Charles's murder shocked the entire nation. President Franklin D. Roosevelt expressed his grief and demanded the killer be caught. Dozens of federal agents converged on the area and searched for clues. The Department of Justice issued a $10,000 reward for information leading to the capture of his killer or killers.

Little Charles was buried on January 13 with a blanket of gardenias covering his coffin. The murder of Charles Mattson was followed by years of rumors and false leads, but his killer was never caught. The case remains unsolved today.

21

The Lady in the Lake (1938)

On a July day in 1940, two fishermen on Lake Crescent were shocked by the sight of a small white hand poking up from the water's surface. The sad story that unfolded following this discovery became one of the most enduring legends in the history of the Olympic Peninsula.

They had found the body of a woman, her features unrecognizable. Someone had beaten her savagely, knocking out her two front teeth. Bruises on her throat showed that she had been strangled. She had been in the water for some time, weighed down in an effort by her murderer to hide the crime. The ropes attached to the weights had gradually disintegrated, and she had floated to the surface. Due to a process known as saponification, her exposed facial features had become soap-like, which is what fed into sensationalized headlines when the story got out, and eventually evolved into the stuff of legends.

For authorities trying to figure out who she was, there were not many clues. She had a large bunion on her foot and a partial dental plate. Several skilled investigators took on the case, including criminologist Hollis B. Fultz, Sheriff Charles Kemp, and Prosecuting Attorney Ralph Smyth. Fultz had previously worked on the two high-profile kidnapping cases of George Weyerhaeuser and Charles Mattson.

They photographed the dental plate from several angles and sent it out to dental magazines across the country with a request for anyone who recognized it to contact them. They also sent a description of the woman to unions and other organizations that might have kept records of employees.

It took a full year, but in August 1941, they finally received a reply that led to the woman's identification. Edgar Thompson, secretary of the Culinary Alliance of Port Angeles, wrote to say that the description sounded like Hallie Illingworth. She was a member of that union and had worked as a waitress at the Lake Crescent Tavern (today's Lake Crescent Lodge). Hallie had failed to show up for work one day back in 1938, and they had never heard from her again.

Kemp and Fultz tracked down a sister of Hallie's, who told them the family had not seen or heard from her for a couple of years. She confirmed that Hallie had a large, painful bunion on one of her feet from years working as a waitress. Another sister remembered the name of a dentist who had done considerable dental work for Hallie, Dr. A. J. MacDonald, of Faulkton, South Dakota. The investigators sent him their pictures of the dental plate and he responded immediately that it was indeed the one he had made for Hallie, whose name at that time was Hallie Spraker; they had identified the body found in the lake.

Five years earlier, on June 16, 1936, Hallie Spraker had married her third husband, a beer truck driver named Monty Illingworth, who was about ten years her junior. They made their home in Port Angeles.

Monty had also been married before and had a young child with that wife. A couple months after his marriage to Hallie, he was arrested in Long Beach, California, for non-payment of child support. He spent some months in prison and after his release began complying with his support orders. However, his rehabilitation only lasted a couple of months before he stopped making payments.

Meanwhile, Monty and Hallie had a volatile relationship. Neighbors reported hearing loud fights, and more than once, Hallie went to work sporting bruises on her face and body. It was not long before Monty met and started a romantic relationship with another woman—and this time he had landed himself a lumber heiress.

Ironically, Monty probably met his new love interest through Hallie. One of Hallie's sisters also lived in Port Angeles, and her flat mate was Elinore Pearson, the daughter of a local lumber magnate. Elinore's father, Petrus Pearson, was one of the wealthiest men in Clallam County. He was general manager of the Crescent Logging Company and of the Port Angeles Western Railroad Company. He lived in a fine home known as the "Airplane House" at 101 E. Fifth Street in Port Angeles. The house is now known as the Peace House.

Elinore Pearson had been married to a bookkeeper for a logging company, probably her father's. The marriage had failed, and she was working as a stenographer and living with Hallie's sister.

Hallie Illingworth had disappeared at Christmas 1937. At the time, Monty's relationship with Elinore was already well-established. After Hallie's disappearance, he left the Olympic Peninsula for Long Beach, California, and Elinore soon followed. Monty told others he didn't know where Hallie was, and that she had run off with another man. Five months later, he filed for divorce from Hallie, citing incompatibility.

In California, Monty and Elinore were in rough financial straits and worked passing out political handbills. It's evident that Elinore's father was not contributing to their maintenance. Elinore later worked for political campaigns, including congressmen and assemblyman. Monty found work as a bus driver and reportedly gave up his carousing and womanizing lifestyle.

The couple lived at 1361 St. Louis Avenue in Long Beach, telling others that they were married. At one point, both of them took time off work and their friends surmised that they were off making their marriage "official." However, Monty's divorce from Hallie had not been finalized, a fact he apparently did not share with Elinore. It was a point that quickly became moot with the discovery of Hallie's body.

Meanwhile, Fultz and the other investigators in Clallam County were looking for Monty. It seemed everyone they interviewed had heard a different story from him about what had happened to Hallie. He told some that she had run off with a sailor; to others, he said she went to Alaska. To one person, he said she moved to Bremerton. To another, he said she went back to her mom in Minneapolis. Still others were told he did not know where she was.

To detectives investigating the murder of Hallie Illingworth, Monty quickly climbed to the top of the suspects list. They soon tracked him down, and on October 24, 1941, they arrived at his door in Long Beach and placed him under arrest.

Initially, the charges against Monty were bigamy. Interestingly, Elinore told them that she and Monty had gotten married at Ellensburg, Washington, on September 3, 1937, which was not only before his incomplete divorce from Hallie but before Hallie's disappearance.

During his initial interview, Monty gave a muddled narrative to detectives that did not make much sense. However, he soon came up with a clearer story describing what had happened the night Hallie disappeared—December 21, 1937.

He said that he had gone to a party with a friend, Tony Enos. They stayed out boozing all night. He came home the next day still drunk and feeling boisterous. Hallie was so mad she left the house and never came back.

Police contacted Tony Enos who confirmed the party and the date. He said he dropped Monty off at 3:30 a.m., which did not match Monty's version of events. He also said that he saw Monty the next morning at around 9 a.m. in Port Angeles near a bank. At that time, Monty told Enos that he was taking Hallie to the Port Ludlow ferry.

As the circumstantial evidence piled up, police officially charged Monty Illingworth with the pre-meditated murder of his wife, Hallie Illingworth. Illingworth was brought to trial in Clallam County on February 24, 1942. The prosecution asked for the death penalty. Despite the fact that the Japanese had bombed Pearl Harbor less than three months earlier and the U.S. had entered World War Two, the Illingworth trial generated giant headlines.

The prosecuting attorney was Max Church, who, ironically, had represented Monty for his divorce from Hallie. His opening statement outlined the case he would make that Monty had planned to murder Hallie. "Church, now the prosecuting attorney, says that the motive can be found in the fact that Monty J. Illingworth wanted to marry Elinore Pearson, the daughter of a rich man, younger and more attractive than Hallie who was ten years older than Monty."[1]

Church outlined his case in his opening arguments:

The conclusion of the prosecution is that Monty J. Illingworth strangled his wife to death in the Guy Apartments, in which they were then living, sometime between three and six in the morning of Wednesday, December 22. He probably immediately wrapped and tied the body in two blankets, in which she was carried from the house and placed in the trunk of the 1937 model sedan, which Illingworth then owned. She was weighted and thrown into the lake.

The cold water practically refrigerated the body until it was found months later. The body came to the surface after the rope had rolled away from the weight. The charge is based largely on the time element proving that he was the last person to have seen his wife alive and that no one but himself had opportunity to kill her.[2]

Church presented a broad circumstantial case against Monty Illingworth, built around his behavior before and after Hallie's disappearance, plus his weak alibi. However, detectives had also pinned down some vital forensic evidence.

Investigators had located Mrs. Harry Brooks, owner of a general store near Monty's home. She recalled that just before Christmas 1937, Monty had borrowed a piece of rope from her. She remembered because he had never paid for the rope nor returned it. She still had the rest of the rope, which allowed scientists to compare her rope with the rope used to bind Hallie's body. The rope fibers were a match.

The defense built their case around the assertion that the lady in the lake was not Hallie at all, but that Hallie was an unfaithful wife who had run off with another man. They produced witnesses who swore they had seen her after the day of her supposed death. However, cross-examination by the prosecution reportedly undercut this testimony.

The defense also produced "scientists" who questioned the detailed testimony from Hallie's former dentist, who had travelled from North Dakota to testify for the prosecution. Observers said that the dentist's testimony was highly convincing. The jury obviously agreed, although they did not return the verdict that the prosecution wanted. They found Monty Illingworth guilty of second-degree murder.

They had settled on the lesser charge because of considerable testimony given by neighbors and friends describing the volatility of the relationship between Monty and Hallie. Ironically, the fact that Monty used to beat Hallie to the point where she went to work with obvious injuries meant to the jury that he had probably killed her in a fit of passion rather than in a premeditated manner. This saved his life.

Although Monty continued to insist that it was "all a mistake," the court sentenced him to life in prison and deputies hauled him off to Washington State Penitentiary in Walla Walla. There, he served only nine years before being released on parole in 1951.

The following year, Monty married again, this time to Genevieve Green, who was not the daughter of a lumber baron. The pair divorced in 1967 and Monty Illingworth died in Orange County, California, in 1974.

Endnotes

Chapter 1

1. *Pioneer and Democrat*, February 26, 1858.
2. *Ibid.*

Chapter 2

1. Winfield S. Ebey diary. Winfield Scott Ebey papers, 1849–1919. University of Washington Libraries, Special Collections.

Chapter 3

1. Winter Brothers, by Ivan Doig, p. 8.
2. *Washington Standard*, March 30, 1861.
3. *Washington Standard*, November 2, 1861.
4. *Ibid.*

Chapter 4

1. *Washington Standard*, November 27, 1875.
2. *Seattle Daily Intelligencer*, October 8, 1877.
3. *Seattle Daily Intelligencer*, May 29, 1875.
4. *Ibid.*
5. *Ibid.*
6. *Ibid.*
7. *Daily Post-Intelligencer*, June 5, 1877.

Chapter 5

1. *Times Colonist*, January 7, 1879.
2. Territory of Washington *v.* Phillips, Mary. 1879. File 1070. Washington State Archives Northwest Regional Branch.
3. *Ibid.*
4. *Ibid.*

Chapter 6

1. *Seattle Daily Post-Intelligencer*, November 11, 1886
2. *Seattle Daily Post-Intelligencer*, Saturday March 6, 1886.
3. *Seattle Daily Post-Intelligencer*, March 6, 1886.
4. Miller *v.* Territory of Washington, Supreme Court of The Territory of Washington. February 2, 1888, p. 61.

Chapter 7

1. *Seattle Daily Post-Intelligencer*, December 1, 1892.
2. *Seattle Daily Post-Intelligencer*, October 20, 1893.
3. *The Weekly Republican*, May 22, 1901.
4. *Seattle Star*, May 23, 1901.
5. *Ibid.*
6. *Ibid.*
7. *Ibid.*
8. *Ibid.*
9. *Ibid.*
10. *Seattle Star*, June 24, 1901.
11. *Ibid.*
12. *Seattle Star*, June 26, 1901.
13. *Seattle Star*, June 25, 1901.
14. *Ibid.*
15. *Ibid.*
16. *Seattle Star*, June 27, 1901.

Chapter 9

1. *Seattle Star*, January 1, 1907.
2. *Adams County News*, July 11, 1906.
3. *Ibid.*
4. *Seattle Star*, December 14, 1906.
5. *Ibid.*
6. *Seattle Star*, December 22, 1906.
7. *Seattle Star*, December 31, 1906.
8. *Seattle Star*, January 4, 1907.
9. *Seattle Star*, January 12, 1907.
10. *Washington Standard*, January 17, 1907.
11. *Seattle Star*, May 20, 1908.

Chapter 10

1. *Seattle Star*, September 26, 1907.
2. *Seattle Star*, July 7, 1908.

Chapter 11

1. *Seattle Star*, June 24, 1909.
2. *The Oregonian*, August 9, 1911.

Chapter 12

1. *Seattle Star*, March 4, 1915.
2. *Seattle Star*, March 5, 1915.
3. *Ibid.*
4. *Ibid.*

Chapter 13

1. *Seattle Star*, July 25, 1916.
2. *Seattle Star*, July 26, 1916.
3. *Seattle Star*, March 8, 1917.

Chapter 14

1. *Seattle Star*, April 19, 1917.
2. *Ibid.*
3. *Seattle Star*, May 2, 1917.
4. *Ibid.*
5. *Ibid.*
6. *Ibid.*

Chapter 15

1. *Seattle Star*, March 20, 1919.
2. *Ibid.*
3. *Seattle Star*, March 21, 1919.
4. *Seattle Star*, March 22, 1919.
5. *Seattle Star*, May 6, 1919.
6. *Seattle Star*, May 7, 1919.
7. *Seattle Star*, May 8, 1919.
8. *Ibid.*
9. *Seattle Star*, May 9, 1919.
10. *Ibid.*
11. *Seattle Star*, June 7, 1919.
12. *Ibid.*
13. *Ibid.*

Chapter 16

1. *Seattle Star*, January 19, 1922
2. *Seattle Star*, January 30, 1922.
3. *Seattle Star*, February 1, 1922.
4. *Ibid.*
5. *Seattle Star*, February 1, 1922.
6. *Ibid.*
7. *Ibid.*
8. *Seattle Star*, February 2, 1922.
9. *Seattle Star*, February 3, 1922.
10. *Ibid.*

11. *Ibid.*
12. *Ibid.*
13. *The Oregonian*, February 5, 1922.
14. *Ibid.*
15. *Ibid.*
16. *Ibid.*

Chapter 18

1. *Seattle Star*, December 22, 1921.
2. *Seattle Star*, September 4, 1922.
3. *Seattle Star*, September 7, 1922.
4. *Ibid.*
5. *Ibid.*
6. *Ibid.*
7. *Ibid.*
8. *Seattle Star*, September 11, 1922.
9. *Ibid.*
10. *Seattle Star*, September 12, 1922.
11. *The Oregonian*, January 12, 1923.
12. *The Oregonian*, January 13, 1923.
13. *The Oregonian*, January 14, 1923.

Chapter 19

1. "Erland's Point murders are committed on March 28, 1934," by Daryl C. McClary. HistoryLink.org Essay 5558.
2. *The Oregonian*, December 15, 1935.

Chapter 20

1. *The Oregonian*, May 27, 1935.
2. *The Evening Star*, May 29, 1935.
3. *The Evening Star*, June 2, 1935.
4. *Evening Star*, July 18, 1935.
5. *Evening Star*, January 3, 1937.
6. *Evening Star*, January 10, 1937.
7. *Ibid.*
8. *The Oregonian*, January 14, 1937.

Chapter 21

1. *Long Beach Independent*, October 31, 1941.
2. *San Antonio Light*, May 17, 1942.

Bibliography

Newspapers

The Aberdeen Democrat
Aberdeen Herald
Adams County News
The Alaska Prospector
Anadarko Daily Democrat
The Athena Press
The Bisbee Daily Review
Bonney Lake-Sumner Courier-Herald
Capital Journal
Cascadia Weekly
Cayton's Weekly
The Coeur d'Alene Press
Colfax Gazette
The Columbian
The Colville Examiner
The Cordoba Daily Times
Corvallis Gazette
The Corvallis Times
Creston News Advertiser
The Daily Alaskan
Daily Alta California
Daily British Colonist
Daily Capital Journal
The Daily Colonist
Daily East Oregonian
The Daily Independent
The Daily Morning Astorian
The Evening Herald
The Evening Journal
The Evening Standard
The Evening Star

The Evening Statesman
The Evening Times
The Great Falls Tribune
Iditarod Pioneer
Kitsap Sun
The Leavenworth Echo
The Lewiston Evening Teller
Long Beach Independent
The Los Angeles Herald
The Lynden Tribune
Madera Tribune
The Morning Astorian
New England Farmer
New York Clipper
The Newport Miner
The Northern Star
Oakland Tribune
Ogden Standard Examiner
Oklahoma County News
The Olympian
The Oregonian
Orleans Independent Standard
The Oroville Weekly Gazette
Pioneer and Democrat
Port Townsend Leader
Puget Sound Courier
Puget Sound Herald
Puget Sound Mail
Puget Sound Weekly Argus
The Richmond Palladium
The Sacramento Union
San Antonio Express
San Antonio Light
San Bernardino Sun
The Salt Lake Tribune
The San Francisco Call
The San Juan Islander
The Santa Fe New Mexican
The Seattle Daily Post-Intelligencer
The Seattle Republican
Seattle Star
Seattle Times
The Spokane Press
The Tacoma Times
The Times-News
Topeka Daily Capital
Vancouver Daily World
The Vancouver Independent
Virginia Chronicle
Washington Standard
The Weekly Republican
The Wenatchee Daily World

Whidbey News-Times
Wichita Daily Eagle
Wilmington Morning Star
The Yakima Herald

Journals

Banel, F., "Chief Leschi lives on 160 years after his execution," retrieved from
mynorthwest.com/900350/chief-leschi-nisqually-tribe/ (February 14, 2018).

Caldbick, J., "Nisqually Chief Quiemuth is murdered in Olympia on November 19,
1856," retrieved from historylink.org/File/10007 (January 18, 2012)

Carpenter, C. V., "Leschi, Last Chief of the Nisquallies," *The Pacific Northwest Forum*,
vol. 1. Number 1, pp. 4–10 (Cheney, Washington: Eastern Washington University,
1976)

Committee to Exonerate Chief Leschi, in cooperation with the Leschi Descendants
(Tacoma: Washington State Historical Society, 2004)

Historylink.org staff, "Native Americans rebury Chief Leschi on tribal land on July 4,
1895," retrieved from historylink.org/File/5480 (July 3, 2003).

McClary, D. C. "Erland's Point murders are committed on March 28, 1934," retrieved
from historylink.org/File/5558 (March 3, 2003).

O'Connell, E., "Who Killed Quiemuth?" Retrieved from thurstontalk.com/2016/01/10/
quiemuth-murder-history/(2016, January 10).

Overton, J., 'The Battle of Port Gamble,' *Columbia: The Magazine Of Northwest History*,
vol. 29, Number 1, pp 23–26 (Tacoma: Washington State Historical Society, 2015)

Winton, N. M., and Corliss, G. W., 'The Death of Colonel Isaac N. Ebey, 1857', The
Pacific Northwest Quarterly, vol. 33, Number 3, pp. 325–347 (Seattle: University of
Washington, 1942)

Historical Documents

James Gilchrist Swan papers, 1833–1909. Special Collections University of Washington
Libraries

Miller *v.* Territory of Washington, 3 Wash. Terr. 554 (1888). Supreme
Court of The Territory of Washington. February 2, 1888. courts.mrsc.org/
territoryreports/003TerritoryReport/003TerritoryReport0554.htm

Territory of Washington *v.* Charles Howard. File 499. Washington State Archives
Northwest Regional Branch

Territory of Washington *v.* Charles Howard. File 686. Washington State Archives
Northwest Regional Branch

Territory of Washington *v.* Phillips, Mary. 1879. File 1070. Washington State Archives
Northwest Regional Branch

Territory of Washington *v.* Quail, Henry; Sutton, Henry L. 1872. File 723 ½.
Washington State Archives Northwest Regional Branch

Territory of Washington *v.* Sutton, Henry L. 1877. File 110. Washington State Archives
Northwest Regional Branch

Territory of Washington *v.* Sutton, Henry L. 1877. File 1033. Washington State Archives
Northwest Regional Branch

Territory of Washington *v.* Sutton, Henry L. 1877. File 1042. Washington State
Archives Northwest Regional Branch

Treaty of Neah Bay, 1855. goia.wa.gov/tribal-government/treaty-neah-bay-1855

Winfield Scott Ebey papers, 1849–1919. University of Washington Libraries, Special
Collections

Books

Baldasty, G. *Vigilante Newspapers* (University of Washington Press: Seattle, 2005)

Doig, I., *Winter Brothers, A Season at the Edge of America (Harvest: Irvine, California, 1982)*

Goodman, L. *Singing the Songs of My Ancestors: The Life and Music of Helma Swan, Makah Elder* (University of Oklahoma Press: Norman, 2003)

McCurdy, J., *By Juan De Fuca's Strait: Pioneering Along the Northwestern Edge Of the Continent* (Binford & Mort Publications: Hillsborough, Oregon, 1937)

Morgan, M., and Gwinn, M. *Skid Road: An Informal Portrait of Seattle* (University of Washington Press: Seattle 1982)

Olsen, G., *Starvation Heights: The True Story of an American Doctor and the Murder of a British Heiress* (Warner Books: New York, 1997)

Vickers, M., *The Architecture of Seattle's Historic Prostitution Trade: Seattle Vice and the Sweet Painted Lady Commerce* (New Jersey: Marquis Publishing, 2017)